TRADITIONS IN TRANSITION:
Jewish Culture in Philadelphia,
1840 - 1940

An exhibition in the museum of
The Balch Institute for Ethnic Studies

Co-sponsored by the Federation of
Jewish Agencies of Greater Philadelphia

Edited by Gail F. Stern

April 24 - October 21, 1989

*The exhibition catalogue is generously supported by grants from
the Pennsylvania Council on the Arts and the Samuel S. Fels Fund.
Distributed by arrangement with AASLH Library,
4720 Boston Way, Lanham, Maryland 20706*

TABLE OF CONTENTS

1 PREFACE M. Mark Stolarik

2 FOREWORD Robert P. Forman

3 ACKNOWLEDGEMENTS

6 INTRODUCTION Gail F. Stern

10 A CENTURY OF TRANSFORMATION: Maxwell Whiteman
Philadelphia Jewry, 1840-1940

28 *IN A COMMON CAUSE, IN THIS* Hannah Kliger
NEW FOUND COUNTRY:
Fellowship and Farein in
Philadelphia

46 *IT USED TO BE LIKE JERUSALEM:* Rakhmiel Peltz
Portal to the City and Enduring
Jewish Community

64 REFLECTIONS OF THE COMMUNITY: Elizabeth Holland
Through the Eyes of
Jewish Photographers

82 CHECKLIST

119 COLOR PLATES

THE BALCH INSTITUTE FOR ETHNIC STUDIES is pleased to present the exhibition and catalog **"Traditions in Transition: Jewish Culture in Philadelphia, 1840-1940."** As part of its mission to promote greater intergroup understanding, the Institute mounts exhibits that reflect and explain the culture of America's more than 100 ethnic groups.

Jews have been coming to the New World since colonial times and have made a unique contribution to our common culture. By stressing religion, education, industriousness, self-help, and works of charity, American Jews have not only been immensely successful in the United States, but have served as role-models for other ethnic groups. These values and accomplishments are reflected in the Philadelphia community.

The Institute is particularly pleased that the Federation of Jewish Agencies of Greater Philadelphia selected the Balch Library as the official repository of the Federation's Archives Center. This close relationship between Balch and the Federation is mutually advantageous not only from a practical standpoint, but from an educational and aesthetic one as well. The Institute's museum has been able to draw upon the Federation's extensive collection to present this comprehensive exhibition on the variety of the Jewish experience in Philadelphia between 1840 and 1940. The Balch-Federation relationship serves as a model that other ethnic groups may wish to emulate.

M. Mark Stolarik
President

"TRADITIONS IN TRANSITION: Jewish Culture in Philadelphia, 1840-1940," is the product of a cooperative effort between the Federation of Jewish Agencies and the Balch Institute for Ethnic Studies. FJA was pleased to join with the Institute in creating this exhibition, based substantially on the Philadelphia Jewish Archives Center's collections. Supplemented by loans from museums, historical societies, synagogues, libraries, local organizations and individuals, the exhibition is the first major presentation locally of its type. It marks another milestone in the years of cooperation between Federation and Balch.

Begun in 1974 as a joint project between Federation and the American Jewish Committee, the Archives collects, preserves and makes available to researchers and the general public the greater Philadelphia Jewish community's records. Included among its collections are records of Jewish organizations, welfare agencies and schools, dating back to the early nineteenth century, memoirs, family histories, photographs, memorabilia, and artifacts.

Before relocating to The Balch Institute in February, 1985, the Archives was quartered in the old Curtis Publishing Company building at Seventh and Walnut Streets. Today the Archives' holdings are complemented by Balch's records on national Jewish life, including Yiddish literature and many books on American Jewish history.

We offer you a special welcome to this exhibit which visually reinforces the collaborative relationship enjoyed by the institutions. We look forward to many more years of cooperation between Federation and Balch and further progress in the preservation of the Jewish community's irreplaceable records.

Robert P. Forman
Executive Vice-President
Federation of Jewish Agencies
of Greater Philadelphia

ACKNOWLEDGEMENTS

THE MUSEUM IS INDEBTED to a great many people who helped us to develop and present "Traditions in Transition." We are grateful to our co-sponsor, the Federation of Jewish Agencies of Greater Philadelphia, and members of its staff, especially Robert P. Forman, Richard Sipser, Rosalie Palan and Lee Leopold. The exhibition would not have been possible without the guidance and generous support of the Exhibition Committee, a subcommittee of the Advisory Board of the Philadelphia Jewish Archives Center at The Balch Institute (PJACBI), chaired by Leon Perelman: Doris and Sid Beshunsky, Maurie Orodenker, Susan A. Popkin (Museum of Judaica of Rodeph Shalom Synagogue), Ernst Presseisen (History Department, Temple University), Diane King (Central Agency for Jewish Education), Seymour Mandelbaum (City Planning, University of Pennsylvania), Edward W. Rosenbaum, M. Mark Stolarik (The Balch Institute for Ethnic Studies) and Edwin Wolf 2nd (Librarian Emeritus, Library Company of Philadelphia). Additional financial support was provided for the exhibition by Sylvan Cohen, Rose Landy, Harry Waber and Charles Kahn, Jr. for Pi Tau Pi Fraternity. The catalog was funded by grants from the Samuel S. Fels Fund and the Pennsylvania Council on the Arts, a state agency. PCA Program Officer David Stephens offered useful advice and help.

I am especially grateful to museum volunteer Ruth Leppel, who served as Associate Curator for the exhibition. Her extensive networking with community organizations, individuals and families contributed to the richness and variety of items included in the exhibition. I am also indebted to Lily Schwartz, PJACBI archivist, for her excellent advice, curatorial assistance and informed knowledge of the collections. Elizabeth Holland of the museum staff, Rutgers University intern Teresa Perkins, Michael Di Pietro of the PJACBI staff, and museum volunteer Leon Leppel also offered invaluable research assistance and help in identifying, documenting and interpreting the artifacts, manuscripts and photographs included in the exhibition.

A special word of thanks is due historian Maxwell Whiteman. In addition to contributing an essay to this publication which provides a historical overview of Jewish immigration to Philadelphia, he generously offered advice and wisdom, as well as curatorial and editorial help throughout all stages of the project. Essayists Hannah Kliger (Department of Judaic Studies, University of Massachusetts) and Rakhmiel Peltz (Research Associate, YIVO Institute for Jewish Research) also provided critical guidance in the selection and interpretation of exhibit materials.

To supplement the PJACBI collections and the Institute's museum and library collections, we relied on numerous, diverse sources for loans. We appreciate the guidance of the staffs of the lending institutions: Dr. Nathan M. Kaganoff, American Jewish Historical Society; Robert Eskind and Jeffrey Ray, Atwater Kent Museum; Penny Balkin Bach and Naomi Nelson, Fairmount Park Art Association; Kay Pyle, Samuel S. Fels Fund; Geraldine Duclow, Free Library of Philadelphia; Jack Weinstein, Gratz College Library; Carolyn Park, Historical Society of Pennsylvania; Kenneth Finkel and Susan Oyama, Library Company of Philadelphia; Gretchen Worden, Ann Vaughn, and Kim Tieger, Mutter Museum of the College of Physicians; Kenneth Libo, David Zipkin, Freya Koss and Sallie Gross, National Museum of American Jewish History; Shawn Aubitz, Nancy Malan and Andrew Dyer, National Archives; Ward Childs, Philadelphia City Archives; Ellen Dunlap, Leslie A. Morris and Kim Rorschach, Rosenbach Museum and Library; Fredric M. Miller and David Weinberg, Urban Archives Center, Temple University; and Pamela Austin and George Brightbill, Photojournalism Collection, Temple University. Board and staff members of beneficial societies and synagogues also graciously helped in securing loans:

Hannah Sinauer, B'nai B'rith International; Morty Naiman, B'nai B'rith Cherry Hill; Lena Sher, Boslover Ahavas Achim Belzer Association; Judy Maslin, Congregation Keneseth Israel; Susan A. Popkin, Museum of Judaica of Congregation Rodeph Shalom; Florence Finkel and Maxwell Whiteman, Congregation Mikveh Israel of Philadelphia; and Rabbi Ivan Caine and Evelyn Segal, Society Hill Synagogue.

Many individuals and families have shared items from their homes and businesses: John Orlando (Arch Sewing Machine Company), the Auspitz Family (Famous 4th Street Delicatessen), the Taxin Family (Old Original Bookbinder's Restaurant), Dr. and Mrs. Daniel Blumberg, Pauline Cohen, Ruth Silberstein Cohen, Harry Boonin, the Boonin Family, Stella P. Cotzer, Harriet Joyce Epstein, Miriam B. Grobman, Gladys Gimpel, Terry B. Horowitz, the Graboyes/Segal Family, Rita Landau, Lee Leopold, Ruth Leppel, Clare Lewin, Mr. and Mrs. Frank P. Louchheim, Seymour Mednick, Bennett and Mildred Merion, Herbert and Cyrel Moser, Joseph Nettis, Mrs. Bert Orodenker, Edward W. Rosenbaum, Ernest Schwartz, Isaac Sherman, T. Sara Slutzky, Sylvia Stein, Mrs. Norma Tarnoff, Anna Weinstein, Maxwell Whiteman, Ruth and Ben Wolf, and Alex Wollod. Donors of Balch museum and library materials represented in the exhibition include: Albert Einstein Medical Center, Betty Ewen, Mrs. Bertha Greenberg, Mrs. Harry M. Hyman, Ruth Leppel, Mrs. Philip Miller, Anna Paull and Etta Paull Aronowitz, Jennie and Judy Rotman, Sylvia Silver, Tom Sroka, Mr. and Mrs. Patrick J. Stanton, Sr., Eileen Voight, Florence Weiner, Workmen's Circle (Philadelphia District), and Eleni Zatz. PJACBI Donors include the Association for Jewish Children, Harriet Baskin, Ben Beitchman, Hannah Green Bergman, Mr. and Mrs. Harry Block, Harriet Braunfield, Miriam Zevin Brillman, Bea Creamer, David Cylinder, Edith Deicht, Eleanor De Vadetsky, Anna Domsky, Federation of Jewish Agencies, Mollie G. Fischer, Frieda

Englander Flick, Louis and Bertha Gershenfeld, Eleanor Gilbert, Anne Green, Anna Harris, Hebrew Charitable Fund, Hebrew Immigrant Aid Society, Mrs. Abraham Hofferman, International Ladies' Garment Workers Union, Jewish Publication Society, Archibald A. Kalish, Sondra Katz, Jerome Keiser, Fran Kleiner, Judge Isador Kranzel, Gella Kraus, Labor Zionist Alliance, Clara Leftwich, Manuel F. Lisan, Manfried Mauskopf, Dr. Sylvester Miller, Mr. and Mrs. Harry Moss, Hyman Myers, Neighborhood Centre, Mrs. Leon Obermayer, Pearl B. Olanoff, Rakhmiel Peltz, Anne Prince, Prushin-Shershow Beneficial Association, Samuel Rabinovitz, Dr. David Rothman, Jennie and Judy Rotman, Edith Satanoff, Ernest Schwartz, Esther Shapiro, Silvia Silver, Anne Smilowitz, William Sobel, William B. Soble, Edith Levin Stern, Ben Sturman, Mrs. Albert Toll, Isadore Trachtenberg, United Hebrew Schools and Yeshivas, William Uris, Mona Weinberg, Edwin Wolf 2nd, and David Zinkoff.

Others who assisted in the preparations for the exhibition include Associate Curator Pamela B. Nelson of the museum staff; Museum Secretary Rosalie M. Robinson; Balch Library Director R. Joseph Anderson and Reference Librarian Patricia Proscino Lusk; library volunteer Gary Unger (who provided Yiddish translations); Balch Education Director James F. Turk; Museum Educator Dolores Healy; Loretta Gunn; and Phyllis Halpern.

Balch Exhibition Designer Steven Tucker created the superb design for the installation, and crafted it with his accustomed skill, ingenuity and patience. Charles Adams, Gregory Zeitlin, and Susan Fisher ably assisted Tucker in the show's fabrication and installation.

Finally, I want to express appreciation to Joan Guerin, who designed this attractive catalog and the accompanying exhibition announcement and to Will Brown, who did the photography for the catalog (with several exceptions noted in the captions). Paula Benkart deserves special credit for her skillful copy editing. Dave Marshall of Keener Offset (Lancaster, PA) offered guidance and assistance in catalog production.

Gail F. Stern

Right:
Programme of Ceremonies at the unveiling of "Religious Liberty" (Checklist #222)

THE BALCH INSTITUTE FOR ETHNIC STUDIES and the Federation of Jewish Agencies had a dual purpose in organizing "Traditions in Transition: Jewish Culture in Philadelphia, 1840-1940." First, we wanted to document the rich and varied social history of the city's Jewish population during a critical period of adaptation and innovation. Second, we wanted to introduce students, scholars, the Jewish community and all others interested in ethnic studies and the city's history to the materials available at the Balch library and museum and at the Philadelphia Jewish Archives Center at the Balch Institute (PJACBI)—a valuable resource administered jointly by the Federation and the Balch library.

In the process of documenting Jewish social, cultural, economic, political, and family life we discovered an enormous wealth of resources not only in the Institute's and the Archives' collections but in the larger community as well. The National Museum of American Jewish History, the Atwater Kent Museum, the Library Company of Philadelphia, the Historical Society of Pennsylvania, the Rosenbach Museum and Library, the Free Library of Philadelphia, Gratz College Library and the Urban Archives Center at Temple University all offer instructive and accessible materials for documenting Jewish social history. In addition, many local synagogues preserve their own manuscript records and maintain collections of historical artifacts. We had space for only a sampling of these, from the Museum of Judaica of Congregation Rodeph Shalom and from Congregation Mikveh Israel, Congregation Keneseth Israel and Society Hill Synagogue. Jewish beneficial societies are still active in Philadelphia, and the Boslover Ahavas Belzer-Bessarabia Association has maintained extensive records, many of which were recently donated to PJACBI. Many families and individuals who learned of the exhibition through newspaper articles or word-of-mouth dug into basements or attics or removed family photographs from their walls, providing greater depth and richness to the show. We hope that the discoveries made in the process of assembling this exhibition will lead to the identification and preservation of additional treasures representing the city's Jewish legacy.

Left:
Boonin family in Slutzk, Russia (Checklist #14)

"Traditions in Transition" is the most recent in a series of social history exhibitions organized by the museum since 1976. Some, including "Irish Eyes Still Smiling" (1983), "Italian American Traditions: Family, Work, and Community" (1985), and "Philadelphia African Americans: Color, Class, & Style, 1840-1940" (1988), have focused on local communities. Others, such as "The Japanese American Experience" (1986) and "Armenian Rugs: Fabric of a Culture" (1988), have been national in scope. In all of these exhibits the museum has interpreted the social history of ethnic groups in America from the standpoint of their "material culture". In taking this approach, we have used as

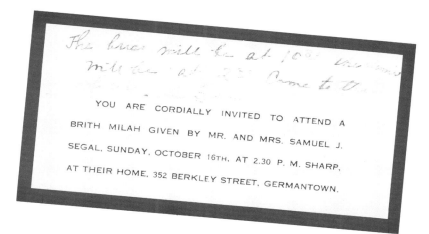

Above:
Invitation to a Brith Milah (Checklist #166)

Above:
Circumcision dress (Checklist #143)

Above:
Sabbath candlesticks from Lithuania (Checklist #12)

"evidence" diaries, journals, letters, correspondence, immigration papers, census documents, organizational records, photographs, published works, clothing, household items, tools, drawings, paintings, sculpture, and other tangible materials created by people that shed light on a subject or theme. The Balch Institute's collections, which consist of library, archival, and museum materials, have served well as points of departure for these exhibitions. In addition, the museum has always worked closely with community groups and organizations in identifying, collecting, and presenting materials which tell their histories.

Above:
Rev. Joseph Krauskopf and a draft of one of his sermons (Checklist #47 and #48)

Right:
Arch Street Theatre sheet music (Checklist #212 and #213)

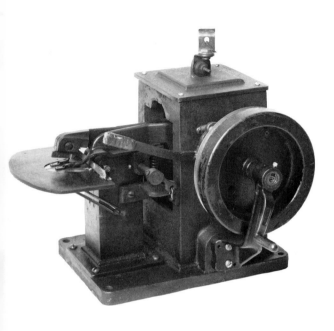

Above:
Buttonhole cutter for men's suits (Checklist #281)

A strong commitment to appropriate, quality design has been another feature of the Institute's exhibits. In any museum show, the visual presentation is as important as the selection and interpretation of objects. In each of our exhibitions the curatorial staff has been fortunate to work closely with a designer in order to develop the format that best presents the concept and content we want to communicate. "Traditions in Transition" continues to put that philosophy into practice.

Numerous books, articles, and essays have been published on the history of the city's Jewish community. We hope that this catalog will make an original contibution to that literature for it contains the fruits of some new research. Maxwell Whiteman not only covers the major "waves" of German and eastern European immigration to Philadelphia, but also discusses immigration from the West Indies and the Levant, subjects rarely addressed in the existing scholarship. Hannah Kliger's article contributes to our knowledge about the number and variety of *landsmanshaftn* (mutual aid societies) that have served the community and evaluates the range of available source materials on the subject. Rakhmiel Peltz presents in his essay the results of extensive field work and original research over nearly a decade in south Philadelphia's Jewish community. Finally, Elizabeth Holland's essay introduces the subject of Philadelphia's Jewish photographers and offers new insights and information on an important aspect of local family and cultural history. In all of these essays the importance of using visual and other forms of documentary source material is evident.

We hope that some of our visitors to the exhibition and readers of the catalog will be encouraged to uncover and preserve additional materials wherever they can be found—whether in family scrapbooks or in the basements of community meeting halls. In this way, the Jewish community's history will continue to unfold.

Gail F. Stern
Museum Director and
Exhibition Curator

MAXWELL WHITEMAN

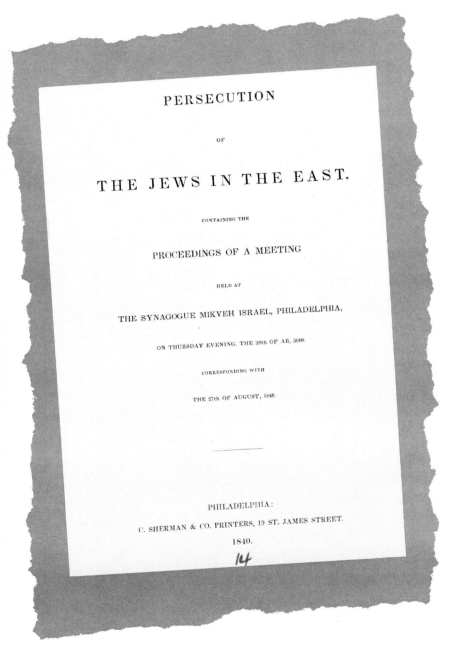

PERSECUTION

OF

THE JEWS IN THE EAST.

CONTAINING THE

PROCEEDINGS OF A MEETING

HELD AT

THE SYNAGOGUE MIKVEH ISRAEL, PHILADELPHIA,

ON THURSDAY EVENING, THE 28th OF AB, 5600.

CORRESPONDING WITH

THE 27th OF AUGUST, 1840.

PHILADELPHIA:
C. SHERMAN & CO. PRINTERS, 19 ST. JAMES STREET.
1840.

THE DECADES WHICH OPEN AND CLOSE the century of Philadelphia Jewish life between 1840 and 1940 were both marked by the intrusion of threatening international events upon the local community. Darkened by the derangement of war and revolution, restrictive laws, economic difficulties, and even famine, masses of Europeans were spurred on to America, resulting in a migration unequaled in modern history. The support Jews received in confronting the danger of anti-Semitism at the beginning of this period was vastly different from the reactions they encountered at the end. Indeed, the responses of Philadelphians and the nation as a whole were as dissimilar as were the city's Jewish communities of 1840 and 1940, after a hundred years of transformation.

At the beginning of the 1840s, the Jewish communities of Europe and the United States were struck by the vile implications of the Damascus case. That notorious incident drew its name from the city where, in February 1840, seven Jews were accused of murdering a priest and using his blood to bake crackers for the Passover holiday. Word of these incredible accusations, which received the support of the governing pashas, spread slowly. Months passed before the news reached American shores, but when it did the press snatched it up like no other similar story since the close of the War of 1812.

Left:
The Persecution of the Jews in the East (Checklist #103)

Less than a year later Isaac Leeser, who as spiritual leader of Mikveh Israel had addressed the Philadelphia audience on the subject of Damascus, turned his efforts to organizing the Jewish congregations of the nation in order to establish an ecclesiastical authority. In addition, Leeser believed such an organization would provide for a system of education, meet the needs of non-English speaking immigrants, and address collateral matters that affected American Jews. Although Leeser's call went unheeded, its significance should not be underestimated, for his dismal failure laid the basis for other antebellum attempts to bring Jews together under a common government.

Left:
Portrait of Isaac Leeser, from Fifty Years' Work of the Hebrew Education Society of Philadelphia (Checklist #229)

Below:
Bilingual edition of the Form of Prayers for Yom Kippur *(Day of Atonement)* (Checklist #28)

The impact of this episode on Christians was remarkable. Spontaneously, they joined Jews in a protest that evoked broad sympathy and nationwide editorial comment. In Philadelphia the Rev. Henry W. Duchachet, Rector of St. Stephen's Episcopal Church, which still stands today on Tenth Street south of Market, gave an impromptu address at Congregation Mikveh Israel; William Ramsey, a Presbyterian clergyman, joined him at the synagogue to condemn Middle Eastern barbarism for subjecting Jews to murder and numerous other atrocities.

Before Jews were able to grasp the enormity of the case, Secretary of State John Forsyth responded to several Jewish congregations that the government of the United States already had issued a protest through its Middle Eastern offices. Ultimately, the imprisoned Jews of Damascus who had survived torture and escaped death were released.

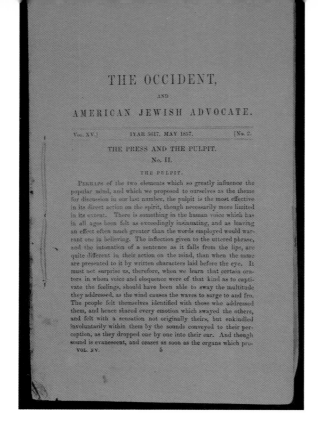

Above:
The first successful English-Jewish journal in the United States
(Checklist #199)

In the spring of 1843 Leeser launched *The Occident,* a monthly journal for American Jews. The success and influence of this pioneer publication remains undervalued but it was a milestone in American journalism. For a quarter century it reflected not only the devotion of one individual, but the thinking of Jews in general as well as their controversies, failures, and achievements. It appealed to the descendants of colonial Jews, attracted the attention of those from the West Indies, and found favor with the Jewish immigrants from Germany who were reaching Philadelphia in greater numbers toward midcentury.

Initially Leeser wrote that Philadelphia's three Jewish congregations comprised a membership of 1800 as compared to the congregations of New York City, which approached 10,000. Whatever the accuracy of these figures, the immigration of Jews from Germany and central Europe increased daily. An examination of approximately 1000 declarations of intent (preliminary citizenship papers) filed in Philadelphia between 1815 and 1860 reveals that the immigrants came from all of the German states though most were from Bavaria, Baden, and Prussia; their rate of literacy was high; and many of them signed their declarations in cursive Hebrew.

In 1881, after forty years of such immigration, Philadelphians could boast twelve synagogues successfully rooted in the community. In addition, there were as many institutions under the Jewish community's auspices. These included a hospital that is today the Einstein Medical Center, an orphans' home, a number of social centers, a private club, and a small chain of independent charitable societies which had developed rapidly in the course of a little more than a decade. One of these, the United Hebrew Charities, founded in 1869, was the forerunner of today's Federation of Jewish Agencies.

All of this was made possible by the efforts of an impoverished, unorganized community largely of immigrant origin that was determined to elevate its economic status and establish institutions to unite the community at least on a secular basis.

From Barbados to Caracas, and from the islands lying between these distant points, yet another wave of Jews was sweeping across the ocean to reach the United States. By 1838 slavery had been abolished in the British West Indies, and the changing economy prompted many of the residents, including Jews, to seek greener fields. Many came to Philadelphia, where they found themselves at complete variance with contemporary emigrants from Germany. Few were economically deprived, and ethnically they were different.

HOSPITAL FOR ISRAELITES
IN PHILADELPHIA.

WHEREAS, A Jewish Hospital has been found to be a necessity in the cities of New York and Cincinnati, and in the large cities of Europe, and

WHEREAS, All the causes that make such an institution a necessity there, are in full operation here, and

WHEREAS, Within the last six months three Israelites of this city have died in Christian hospitals, without having enjoyed the privilege of hearing the שמע ישראל, the watchword of their faith and nation, and

WHEREAS, It reflects the greatest discredit on so large a Jewish population as that of Philadelphia, to force friendless brothers to seek, in sickness and the prospect of death, the shelter of un-jewish hospitals, to eat forbidden food, to be dissected after death and sometimes even to be buried with the stranger.   Therefore be it

Resolved, That the District Grand Lodge No. 3, of the Independent Order of the Benai Berith, acting on that Benevolence and Brotherly Love, which are the motto of the Order, take immediate steps to secure the co-operation of all Jewish societies and individuals for the purpose of founding a Jewish hospital, and be it further

Resolved, That the whole subject be and is hereby refered to a special committee of seven, to be called the Hospital Committee.

In consequence of our appointment as a provisional Committee to promote the founding of a Jewish hospital in or near the city of Philadelphia, at a meeting of the Grand Lodge of the Benai Berith, held on Sunday, the 14th of August, we now appeal to you for your active sympathy and co-operation, to carry out the idea embraced in the above proceedings.

Provisional
Hospital Committee.
{ M. Thalheimer, *Chairman,*
Isaac Leeser, *V. Chairman,*
A. Sulzberger, *Secretary,*
S. Hofheimer,
R. Teller,
L. Ellinger,
S. Weil.

Philadelphia, August 18th, 1864.
Menachem 16th, 5624.

NOTICE.—The Grand Lodge in taking the initiative do not design to forestall public action, but desire to defer the plan to a general meeting of committees from various public bodies and individual Israelites, to be held at the earliest possible date.

Spital für Israeliten
in Philadelphia.

In Erwägung, daß die Gründung jüdischer Spitäler in den Städten New-York und Cincinnati, sowie in den größern Städten Europas sich als Nothwendigkeit herausstellte,

In fernerer Erwägung, daß das Bedürfniß eines solchen Institutes in der hiesigen Stadt eben so dringend ist,

In fernerer Erwägung, daß während der jüngsten sechs Monate, drei hiesige Israeliten in christlichen Spitälern starben, denen der Todeskampf nicht durch Vernehmung der Worte: שמע ישראל erleichtert wurde,

In fernerer Erwägung, daß es einer so zahlreichen jüdischen Bevölkerung wie der Philadelphia's zur großen Unehre gereicht, für ihre verlassenen Brüder während ihrer Krankheit und ihrer Todesstunde nicht zu sorgen, so daß diese unglücklichen Brüder zu nicht-jüdischen Spitälern ihre Zuflucht nehmen, und dort verbotene Speisen genießen müssen, nach ihrem Tode auch oft secirt und auf nicht-jüdischen Begräbnißplätzen beerdigt werden; daher sei es

Beschlossen, Daß die Distrikts-Groß-Loge No. 3, des Unabhängigen Ordens Bene Berith, treu ihrem Wahlspruche der Wohlthätigkeit und brüderlichen Liebe, ungesäumt die nöthigen Schritte thue, um die Mitwirkung aller jüdischen Gesellschaften und Individuen zur Gründung eines jüdischen Spitals zu sichern; und sei es ferner

Beschlossen, Daß der ganze Gegenstand einer Spezial-Committee von sieben, die den Namen „Spital-Committee" führt, übertragen werde, und somit übertragen ist.

In Folge unserer Ernennung, bitten wir Sie, Ihr reges Mitgefühl und Ihre Mitwirkung der Ausführung des vorstehenden Plans zu schenken.

Provisorische
Spital-Committee.
{ M. Thalheimer, Vorsitzer,
Isaac Leeser, V. Vorsitzer,
Abraham Sulzberger, Secretär,
Solomon Hofheimer,
R. Teller,
L. Ellinger,
S Weil.

Philadelphia, den 18ten August, 1864
16ten Menachem, 5624.

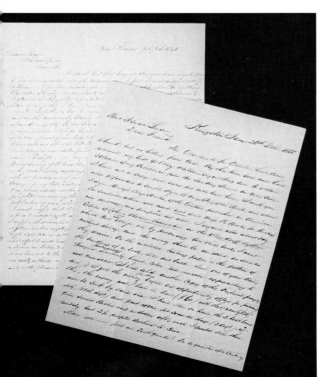

Above:
Notice of the Committee established for the purpose of founding a Jewish Hospital (Checklist #111)

Left:
Letters to Isaac Leeser from Jews in Kingston, Jamaica, 1858 (Checklist #29) *and St. Thomas, 1841. Maxwell Whiteman Collection.*

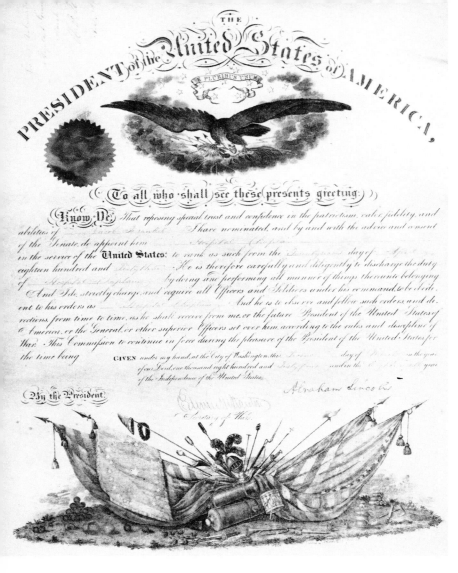

Above:
Civil War Commission of Rev. Jacob Frankel as Hospital Chaplain
(Checklist #107)

Their island culture was new among the Philadelphians, and even though English was their native tongue, many were also fluent in Spanish, French, and Italian and were accomplished in Hebrew. Their names bespoke their diversity: Andrade, Finzi, Lobo, DeCasseres, Sanguinetti, and Ottolenghui. They affliliated themselves with Congregation Mikveh Israel, kept aloof from those of German background, and quietly left their mark on the city of Philadelphia. Today their descendants carry such names as Stein or Bernstein.

Sabato Morais was the link between the immigrants from Germany and those from eastern Europe, as well as a source of comfort to the West Indians. The Italian-born minister of Mikveh Israel who suceeded Isaac Leeser, Morais served the congregation between 1851 and the year of his death in 1897. The Germans turned to him for personal aid. When they lacked work, he outfitted them with novelties or other goods that could be conveniently hawked from baskets on city streets. In the traditional Jewish manner he helped provide for widows and orphans and found lodging for homeless immigrants; he even learned their speech because many spoke and wrote Yiddish, rather than German as commonly believed. Morais' records show him as mentor and guide, as a fountain of human warmth, and as one who discreetly dispensed the congregational charity to accommodate the newcomers.

It was from the pulpit, however, that Morais struck the most significant note in his long career. At Mikveh Israel his discourses, based on biblical teachings, interpreted the tragic course of American history. He was an anti-slavery spokesman, a supporter of Lincoln in a divided congregation, and active in the young Republican party. Rooted in Jewish concepts of social justice, his sermons reached such a fervor and controversial pitch that in 1864 steps were taken to remove him from the pulpit. They failed. In turn, his friends and supporters at Mikveh Israel awarded him a lifetime contract as minister of the city's oldest congregation. During the administration of President Grant, when the rumblings of anti-Jewish conduct in the

Above:
Application of Rebekah Hyneman for Civil War pension of her son Elias,
2 January, 1875
National Archives

Following the Civil War Mikveh Israel still held its leading position in the city. There was something alluring about its title as the Spanish-Portuguese congregation. Even though its membership was constantly reenforced by Iberian descendants, it was Spanish-Portuguese in rite and tradition rather than in ethnic composition. Through its ritual it amalgamated a variety of Jews as no other congregation was able to.

Nevertheless, as a result of internal ethnic disputes, Rodelph Shalom Synagogue emerged as a fragment of Mikveh Israel and Keneseth Israel as a fragment of Rodelph Shalom. Beth Israel, improperly described as a Polish congregation, but in fact one of English-speaking Jews who observed a Polish rite, also broke away from Mikveh Israel after finding the Sephardic ritual unacceptable. The same was true of the last of the secessionist groups, B'nai Israel, the congregation in South Philadelphia which separated from Mikveh Israel in the 1850s, whose members came from Holland. In spite of these secessions, the parent congregation maintained its status quo. The beauty of Mikveh Israel's melodious liturgy is as appealing today as it was when Gershom Mendes Seixas read the prayers during the War of Independence.

Empire of the Tsar reached the United States, Morais reacted at once on behalf of the Russian Jews and from year to year consistently supported the victims of Tsarist pillage and pogrom.

In the meantime, Jews from Philadelphia had served in all of the branches of the armed forces. They were active in the Pennsylvania cavalry units, and had organized their own regiments with support from their congregations. Having fought at Antietam, Sharpsburg, and New Market, Jewish soldiers from Philadelphia died on the battlefield and in Confederate prisons. Their sacrifices inspired the intensive efforts in Philadelphia and throughout the country that led to Jacob Frankel's appointment as the first Jewish chaplain to the armed forces of the United States.

Below:
M. Rosenbaum business card (Checklist #9)

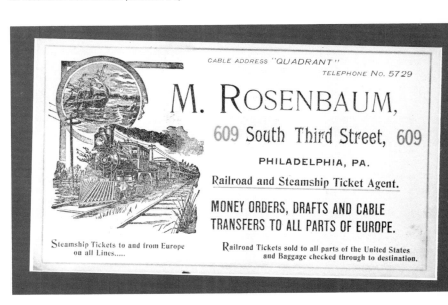

The United Push Cart Peddlers Ass'n

Above:
United Pushcart Peddlers broadside (Checklist #270)

Between the administrations of President Ulysses S. Grant and Woodrow Wilson, Philadelphia Jewry underwent an enormous transformation. From 1884, when the city's Jewish population was estimated at 12,000, to 1907, some 76,000 Jews immigrated directly to Philadelphia. Figures on additional immigrants who reached the city by way of New York, Baltimore, and other ports are purely speculative, and those who left Philadephia to go elsewhere are not fully recorded. By 1940, the close of the period surveyed in this exhibition, however, the estimated Jewish population approached 300,000.

The well-organized charitable societies, educational institutions, and health care programs developed by the Jewish immigrants from Germany and their children were not adequate to meet the needs of the Jews who streamed in from the lands between the Baltic and the Black Seas. In the words of Israel Zangwill, those newcomers were a "peculiar people" in language, habit, and religious practice. Moreover, they had ideas of their own.

The eastern European Jews were eager to establish their own societies based on their home-country values and traditions and eventually did so. But they were dependent upon the existing structure until they could obtain a foothold. To ease this process, Jews of German background established in 1884 the Association for the Protection of Jewish Immigrants. Its purpose was to set up a system for meeting immigrants at the landing station, clearing them through the port of entry, registering their names, providing them shelter and health services, and seeing that they were properly fed.

The leading figure in the new association was Louis Edward Levy, who had come to the United States from Bohemia in 1854, and who subsequently developed the process for printing halftone reproductions in newspapers and other journals. In carrying out the aims of his vast undertaking Levy was fortunate to obtain the services of Moses Klein. A meticulous record keeper and tireless worker adept in most European languages, Klein was named an official interpreter for the local port.

Left:
Charter of Association for the Protection of Jewish Immigrants
(Checklist #24)

Below:
Ships' passenger lists, Association [for the Protection] of Jewish Immigrants (Checklist #1)

17

Above:
Portrait of Mordecai Bateman (Checklist #141)

Right:
Burial records of the Levantine Jews Society (Checklist #36)

Thanks to the effective apparatus created by Levy and Klein, tens of thousands of immigrants entered the country more safely and comfortably than did the hundreds of thousands arriving amidst the helter-skelter conditions of New York City. The Philadelphians established official communication with offices abroad, as well as with major ports in the United States, tackling all the human problems that confronted the uprooted, from locating lost baggage to tracing runaway husbands.

Inner city life also had to be restructured to accommodate the changes in immigration. The needs of immigrants from central Europe could be met on an individual basis by leaders such as Sabato Morais, but the Association had to work closely with other organizations, especially the United Hebrew Charities, to help the throngs from eastern Europe. The Charities had established a number of employment offices, provided various forms of relief, and in a sense pioneered a system of social work. Its annual reports are rich in immigration data and provide information on how the established community approached new and existing problems.

In the midst of this vast immigration came Jews from the Levant and from the entire Ottoman Empire. Lost in the vortex of the eastern Europeans, they have been neglected by historians. Turkish, Syrian, and Lebanese Jews and some from eastern Yugoslavia and Bulgaria seem to have vanished while living in the midst of those from Russia and Poland. Where are the Abulafias and the Abuzeiras today? Their language, Ladino, a mixture of Spanish and Hebrew, was vastly different from that of other Jews. Their foods were Middle Eastern when these foods were unknown in the city and even their Sephardic religious observances varied from the Spanish-Portuguese rite as practiced by Mikveh Israel.

By 1909 there was an unusual ethnic mixture among Philadelphia Jewry. That year Mikveh Israel closed the doors of its Seventh Street synagogue and moved to a more attractive site at Broad and York. At the suggestion of Louis Edward Levy and Reverend Leon H. Elmaleh, the Seventh Street synagogue was reopened as the Free Synagogue for the Levantine Jews and those unaffiliated with the South Philadelphia congregations.

Left:
The Reverend Leon Elmaleh (Checklist #35)

Right:
Charter of The Federation of Jewish Charities of Philadelphia
(Checklist #88)

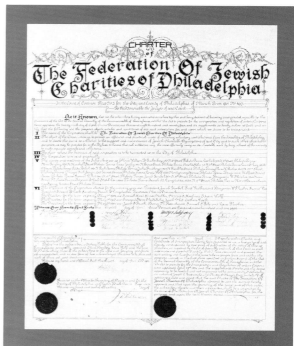

20

Organizing the Jewish community prior to the first World War was a difficult task. The eastern Europeans sought to build their own organizations and establish their own hospital (Mount Sinai), their own foster homes and homes for the aged, and those societies known as *landsmanshaftn*, based on hometown associations and backgrounds. Still other beneficial societies and a variety of lodges assured them mutual aid in sickness and death.

As early as 1891 eastern Europeans sought to form a federation of Jewish organizations to provide funding for their many expanding institutions. The United Hebrew Charities no longer served its purpose and required change. Ten years later the new umbrella group finally came into being under the title of the Federation of Jewish Charities, the forerunner of the present Federation.

To articulate their needs and to express what they thought, the new Yiddish-speaking Jews launched their own press. Between 1892 and 1941, twenty-one newspapers were published; the most successful and influential was the *Yiddishe Velt*. Philadelphia also had an indigenous Yiddish theater and literary group. The Hebrew Literature Society, founded in 1885, was the most important of the city's small but active Hebrew circles, and their warmest supporter was Judge Mayer Sulzberger, savant and communal leader.

The Yiddish press looms large in importance when compared with the *Jewish Exponent*, a weekly newspaper founded in 1887. They were the voices of two separate worlds living side by side. The *Exponent* warned the community about the perpetuation of Yiddish, the jargon tongue of the old ghetto which hindered all progress toward Americanization. But the Yiddish columns contained the first statements on Zionism in Philadelphia as well as portraits of the local Yiddish stage, the rising labor movement, the community's strong religious element and its vocal radical movement. Little of this was present in the *Exponent*.

Nevertheless, the *Exponent* is a major source for the early influence of the German milieu on Philadelphia's Jewish community and its institutional evolution. Just as it is necessary to turn to the Yiddish press for an account of the life of the eastern European immigrants, so it is equally necessary to draw on the *Exponent* for the history of the Jewish communal structure and its development before World War I.

Right:
Playbill for The Golem (Checklist #214)

The Federation of Jewish Charities was the central dependable source for gathering funds to support its various agencies, including the Jewish Hospital, but the Kehillah movement endeavored to bring secular and religious interests into one organization, without intruding on their independence. Its major aim was to further Jewish education in all branches—there already were more than 65 schools serving in excess of 10,000 students. But better control over the preparation and distribution of Kosher food products, especially meat, was essential, as was the need to deal with internal religious disputes. Although the idea first met with favor, the Kehillah movement fell apart because the task of such unification was simply too great.

Right:
Portrait of Hyman Gratz (Checklist #230)

Below:
Brick certificate for the Central Hebrew Free School
(Checklist #240)

However, there is a consistent institutional history that Philadelphians can point to with pride: a Jewish Publication Society that recently celebrated its centennial, the Jewish Theological Seminary, founded in New York in 1886 and the product of Morais' efforts, the Gratz College for training in Hebrew on a higher level and the now defunct Dropsie College, a post-graduate institution devoted to a variety of Semitic studies. While these institutions were still in their infancy at the outbreak of World War I, older, communally supported educational institutions were thriving and attracting children.

The first World War distracted the local focus to problems abroad as Jews were wedged in the conflict between powerful forces. They fought in all the armies of Europe, and when the United States declared war against Germany in 1917, the immigrants donned American uniforms at Ypres and Verdun.

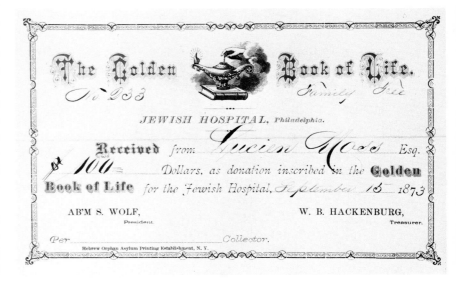

Above:
Receipt for donation by Lucien Moss to The Jewish Hospital
(Checklist #114)

Below:
Schiff Classics Committee, Jewish Publication Society (Checklist #203)

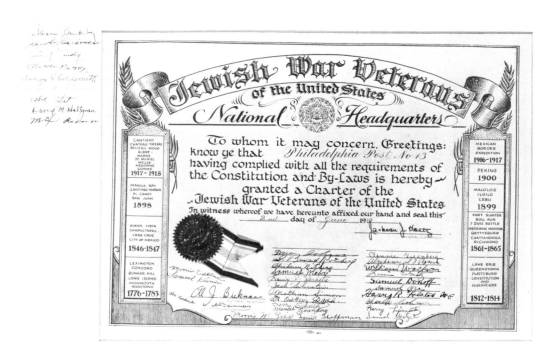

Above:

Charter of Philadelphia Post #13 of the Jewish War Veterans
(Checklist #110)

The war accomplished what the existing immigration laws had failed to do: it curbed immigration. After the war more restrictive legislation limited immigration to a low that particularly hurt Jews. The former Association of Jewish Immigrants was incorporated into the Hebrew Immigrant Aid Society, a major national organization. In the meantime, Jews were entrapped by the Russian revolution and were especially vulnerable in the Ukraine. Whom the Bolshevik armies and the Red Calvary did not destroy, the armies of White Russia eliminated. Those fortunate enough to escape were victimized by Ukrainian pogromists, who themselves were terrorized by fanatical Soviets. The Federation of Jewish Charities sponsored a massive campaign for the relief of the postwar victims and homeless refugees, galvanizing the full force of a community in distress to produce the largest relief effort of its kind since the Kishinev massacres at the beginning of the century.

The twenties heightened the visibility of the two extremes of Philadelphia Jewry. On one hand was the socially elite group that could be seen through the windows of the Locust Club, and on the other was the extremely poor. In between these extremes were restless immigrants and their children who sought their own level of recognition. The twenties marked the beginning of geographical and social rapprochement among the descendants of the German and the eastern European Jews, although old patterns of distrust and disagreement continued to linger. Older neighborhoods began to disintegrate, and second and third areas of settlement grew as Strawberry Mansion, Logan and Wynnefield attracted even greater numbers of Jewish residents out of South Philadelphia. Economic prosperity surged forward; unions among Philadelphia's clothing workers increased in strength, as did the ranks of strikers; (see Color Plate #23) and the number of synagogues in the new areas rose considerably. But grand hopes for a bright future were shattered like an eggshell toward the end of October 1929.

The Great Depression brought more than economic distress to the Jewish community. By 1933 a large but undetermined number had become dependent on the welfare agencies of the Jewish Federation whose funding was frequently on the verge of exhaustion. Employment agencies worked vigorously to find jobs to remove their clients from the rolls of the general welfare societies. But the grip of deprivation would not loosen despite the introduction of Federal programs of assistance. For Jews, however, the worst aspect of the decade was the outbreak of the most virulent anti-Semitism in American history.

In Philadelphia the anti-Jewish invective was unleashed by the voice of Father Charles E. Coughlin, the Catholic "radio priest" broadcasting from Detroit, who had adopted the philosophy of the German-American Bund. A powerful German propaganda machine, the Bund was perhaps stronger in Philadelphia than in other cities. It was led locally by Gerhardt Wilhelm Kunze and published a bilingual newspaper, the *Philadelphia Weckruf and Beobachter*, in addition to distributing the Coughlin newspaper, *Social Justice*. Dressed in uniforms, shouting anti-Jewish slogans, and hawking copies of their newspapers, members successfully spread the message of hate. When Fritz Kuhn, the Bund's national leader, was imprisoned for embezzlement in 1939, Kunze was named his successor.

On November 20, 1938, only a week after the infamous Kristallnacht witnessed the burning of the synagogues and the national desecration of German Jewry, Father Coughlin let loose his first undisguised attack on Jews over a nationwide radio network. He charged that the Jews had invited and deserved their suffering because nazism is a defense mechanism against communism, and communism is Jewish.

Refutations and denials by prominent journalists, historians, and government officials poured fourth immediately, and Catholic and Protestant laymen protested. When it was demonstrated that Coughlin's propaganda was derived from German sources, Philadelphia's radio station WDAS, which carried his broadcasts, demanded that Coughlin henceforth submit the text of any address at least forty-eight hours in advance. Coughlin refused and the station denied him the use of its facilities, prompting Coughlin's followers and sympathizers to organize a yearlong boycott of the local station. As they picketed WDAS, the Coughlinites heaped vile abuse upon Jews and all who condemned Coughlin.

One spectacle followed another. A number of Protestant leaders joined the anti-Jewish crusade and inflammatory addresses warned of the dangers of Jewish intrigue and conspiracy to seize the government of the United States. Small Christian circles and spokesmen for the American Legion condemned these outrages, but their voices were largely unheard. Most churchmen did not deal with the issue at all.

One of the great anti-Semitic spectacles of the 1930s was the "discovery" by William Pelley of a new document in American history, the forged diary of Charles Cotesworth Pinckney. Pelley claimed that at the Constitutional Convention at Philadelphia in 1787 (Pelley used the year 1789), Benjamin Franklin had urged the Convention to exclude the "Asiatic Jews" from the country, and Pelley attributed additional scurrilous statements to Pinckney. Before the forgery could be disproved by Franklin scholars, who showed that Franklin's friendliness toward Jews was expressed in his public support of Philadelphia's Congregation Mikveh Israel, the false document was reprinted and spread across the nation. Americans familiar with their country's history detected the forgery at once, but the widespread ill effects of the calumny were not easily undone. Indeed copies of the forgery were still being circulated as late as 1966.

The 293,000 Jews of the Philadelphia area, slightly less than one-sixth of the City's population, were not organized sufficiently to counterattack the fascists and anti-Semites. The local branches of two national organizations, the American Jewish Congress and B'nai B'rith, mustered their strength in an effort to defend the truth about American and world Jewry. The energies of those two groups were not strongly concentrated in the Philadelphia area, however, and the American Jewish Committee, which also worked in the field of human rights, had no office at all in the city at that time. A national effort to institute a boycott of German imported goods attracted much attention but accomplished very little. Locally the *Jewish Exponent,* still an independent weekly, protested bitterly against the anti-Semitic groups while the less inhibited Yiddish press clamored for an effective organization that would not be limited by the techniques of a defensive philosophy. But secular leadership proved timid and fearful of provoking further incidents of anti-Semitism. Altogether attempts to repudiate German Nazi and Coughlinite propaganda and to disseminate correct information about Jews were not equal to the task.

The few who recognized the world crisis of Jewry were mocked for their pessimism. Refugees fleeing Germany, the last stage in a century of immigration, carried with them copies of the *Philo Atlas,* a guide book for emigrants fleeing the might of German terror. The doors to American freedom were being tightly closed, they found; the traditional dream was for the time dissipated. True, the resurgence of anti-Semitism and the coming of the second World War brought forth remarkable activity among Philadelphia's Jews. The defense agencies mustered new strength; new philanthropic societies flourished where none had existed, and religious institutions approached a hundred or more with rabbinical and congregational societies filling a major gap. Yet it was still impossible to comprehend that the conflagration with which Europe was ablaze in war would consume six million Jews.

Maxwell Whiteman *is the author of ten books in the fields of bibliography and local ethnic and social history. He has contributed to numerous journals on a variety of subjects, and has edited and introduced more than forty volumes of rare Black Americana. Whiteman was responsible for rejuvenating the library and introducing the archival program at the Philadelphia Union League.*

Left:
Handbook for Jewish Emigrants *published in Berlin* (Checklist #27)

Suggested Reading

Annual Reports of the Association of Jewish Immigrants of Philadelphia, 1885- 1919. Philadelphia: Association of Jewish Immigrants of Philadelphia.

The Persecution of Jews in the East, Containing the Proceedings of a Meeting Held at The Synagogue Mikveh Israel. Philadelphia: C. Sherman & Co., Printers, 1840.

Riglamentos Konsirnando La Katigoria . . . (Regulations Concerning Various Categories of Membership). New York: Society of Levantine Jews, 1910 (In Ladino and English).

Whiteman, Maxwell, "The Fiddlers Rejected: Jewish Immigrant Expression in Philadelphia," in *Jewish Life in Philadelphia, 1830-1940,* edited by Murray Friedman. Philadelphia: ISHI Publications, 1983.

_____, *Mankind and Medicine: A History of Philadelphia's Albert Einstein Medical Center.* Philadelphia: Albert Einstein Medical Center, 1966.

_____, "Isaac Leeser and the Jews of Philadelphia," in *Publications of the American Jewish Historical Society,* 48 (June, 1959)

IN A COMMON CAUSE, IN THIS NEW FOUND COUNTRY":
Fellowship and Farein in Philadelphia

HANNAH KLIGER

IMMIGRANT JEWS TO PHILADELPHIA and other American urban centers supported a vast network of organizations that they created by themselves. The most prevalent and innovative of these institutions, however, was the Jewish voluntary association based on its members' shared origins in their eastern European city or town and known in Yiddish as the *farein* or *landsmanshaft.*

Hometown clubs were the vital and creative grass-roots response of a transplanted population. In New York City one of every four Jews belonged to a landsmanshaft in the early decades of the twentieth century.[1] Estimates as to how many thousand such organizations were created are imprecise because the available sources on these mutual aid societies are generally undervalued by their keepers and overlooked by researchers. Nevertheless, by collecting and scrutinizing what one scholar of immigration has termed "diamonds in your own backyard,"[2] the lives of ordinary people can be interpreted from their own records and their own testimony.

In this essay I suggest ways to utilize resources available for the study of Jewish immigrant associations in Philadelphia. Unless otherwise noted, the materials I discuss are from the holdings of the Philadelphia Jewish Archives Center at the Balch Institute for Ethnic Studies. These records show how Jews in the City of Brotherly Love helped themselves and helped others "in a common cause, in this new found country."[3]

Beginning in the 1800s, immigrants created landsmanshaftn in order to pray together, to provide financial assistance and insurance benefits, to offer a traditional burial, and to send aid to the hometown. The organizations also served as social centers for people sharing loyalty to a common birthplace.

The mass migration of Russian Jews to Philadelphia after 1880 prompted action and concern by the city's established Jewish community to "bid the Hebrew welcome here."[4] The immigrants, nonetheless, favored being among their own *landslayt,* the Yiddish term for fellow townspeople, familiar friends and neighbors with whom memories of the old home and anxieties about the new one could be easily shared. In addition, the eastern Europeans correctly surmised that the "older Jewish charities were overburdened and ideologically unprepared to face the immigrants in spite of their willingness to do so."[5]

To be sure, Jewish lodges and fraternal orders existed in the city prior to the influx of Jews from eastern Europe. Before 1880, for example, there were active branches of the Order of B'nai B'rith, Independent Order Free Sons of Israel, Order Kesher Shel Barzel, and Independent Order Sons of Benjamin. The benevolent and charitable features of their work are poetically portrayed in the report of the Works Progress Administration's Ethnic Survey on the Jews of Philadelphia. The "seven boughs of benevolence" that mark organized Philadelphia Jewry are traced to traditional Jewish precepts regarding mutual aid and responsibility.

> *Seven are the branches of the sacred candlestick and seven are the branches of charity first defined in the ancient Land of Canaan and repeated century after century in the writings of the rabbis. To feed the hungry, clothe the naked, visit the sick, bury the dead and comfort the mourners, redeem captives, shelter the homeless, and provide poor maidens with dowries are the commandments of the Jewish community.[6]*

These humanitarian principles were institutionalized in the organizations of their Sephardic and German predecessors as well as in the farein of the eastern European Jews, but the societies whose members shared the more intimate bonds of covillagers in Russia, Poland, or Galicia eventually outnumbered the older ones. Almost every Philadelphia neighborhood experienced a surge in immigrant associations with the aims reflected in the constitution of the Korsoner Farein: (1) to foster friendship and brotherly love among members, (2) to provide burial services for members, (3) to aid the family of deceased members.

For one circle the impetus to band together grew from an informal self-help rite practiced during weekend get-togethers in each others' homes. At their weekend parties the young men and women from Vitebsk passed around a *royter fatsheylke* (red bandana) to collect anonymous contributions to help needy friends. When chartered as the Vitebsker Beneficial Association in 1897, the society broadened its framework to include such official duties as securing burial ground, supporting a relief fund, and distributing donations to various charities in the United States, in Palestine, and in the founders' Belorussian hometown (see Color Plate #22).

Their incorporation as an association did not reduce the importance compatriots placed on the fellowship and friendship which the fatsheylke had symbolized. Indeed, on the occasion of their thirtieth anniversary in 1928 a member of the Vitebsker farein composed a poem to be sung to the melody of the popular Yiddish tune "Rozhinkes mit Mandlen" (Raisins and Almonds), extolling the virtues of camaraderie in what he affectionately called the *sosayete'le* (our dear little Vitebsker society).

In the United States, the first societies of eastern European Jews were typically known as *ansheys* or *chevras* (anshey means "people of"; chevra refers to a congregation). These religious landsmanshaftn formed around a synagogue in addition to providing mutual protection and relief.

The oldest society in this category in Philadelphia, the Chevra Bikur Cholim, founded in 1861, held services on the Sabbath and holidays. From an original core of fifteen men, the organization grew to celebrate its one hundredth anniversary in 1961. In the group's forty-eighth year its in-house journal, *Chevra Bikur Cholim News*, spawned the first issue of the *Jewish Advancer*, a newspaper devoted to the interests of Jewish fraternal societies in Philadelphia.[7]

The second oldest society was the Krakauer Chevra Beth Elohim, formed in 1876 and named for the city of Krakow. Members first secured a place for worship, then united in 1879 with the Krakauer Beneficial Society. The corporate charter they were granted in 1882 as the Krakauer Beth Elohim Society stated their purpose:

> *The worship of Almighty God, according to the orthodox ritual of the Jewish Church; the accumulation of a fund by dues and assessments for the benefit and protection of its members in case of sickness or disability; to provide for the internment of deceased members and member's [sic] wives, and the support of members during any period of mourning and to provide burial lots in case of the death of a member or any of his family.[8]*

In order to qualify for membership it was necessary to be a citizen of Pennsylvania, to be of the Jewish faith, over twenty-one years of age, "and possessed of good character and free from any bodily infirmity."[9] As was common for landsmanshaftn, sons and sons-in-law were recruited as new members and officers, and reportedly some "members of Krakauer refused to consent to their daughter's marriage unless the suitor joined, or promised to join."[10] The society developed various affiliates, such as the Ladies Auxiliary and the Krakauer Federal Credit Union, as well as numerous committees, its own bowling league, and a monthly in-house newsletter.

Landsmanshaft documents such as in-house journals, constitutions, souvenir albums, financial ledgers, and minute books mirror the convergence of age-old Jewish communal values with American protocols. The by-laws of the Krakauer Beth Elohim Beneficial Society, for instance, stipulate appropriate behavior when a member observes the traditional seven days of mourning, namely that "a member keeping *Schiva* (seven days) shall be entitled to *Minjan* (prayer quorum) every evening." In this same text rules of order for decorum at meetings are outlined. "Any member who shall misbehave himself in the meeting . . . shall be admonished," and "no member shall be interrupted while speaking . . . Fines, penalties, and even expulsions (e.g. for "taking sick through immoral conduct") are specified.[11] Records of other synagogue-based landsmanshaftn located mainly in South Philadelphia, including Chevra Ateres Israel Anshe Brahin V'Choimetsh (see Color Plate #24), Congregations Anshei Sdo Lovon, Congregation Tifereth Anshei Zitomir, and the Chevra Ahavas Achim Anshe Nezin follow this model and indicate a similar evolution of priorities and goals.

After 1880 newcomers also began to generate a host of landsmanshaftn to reflect their diverse occupations, political allegiances, and religious views, as well as gender and age differences. The Polish city of Bialystok, to cite just one example, once was represented by over forty separate landsmanshaftn in America, a majority of them in New York, but also including two active lodges in Philadelphia.[12]

The degree of institutional complexity and the extent of diversity among landsmanshaftn that we find in New York is not matched in any other city.[13] Nevertheless, as among Italian immigrants in Philadelphia, where in "an elaborate varied proliferation of 'little Italies' . . . even very small towns could have had several societies,"[14] the city of Philadelphia was to become home to myriad landsmanshaftn of eastern European Jews.

Above:
Officers of the Minsker Young Friends Benevolent Association
Balch Library Collection. Jewish Daily Forward *Papers.*

Left:
*25th Anniversary Banquet program, Zashkover Ladies' Auxiliary
Philadelphia Jewish Archives Center at The Balch Institute. Gift of Judge
Isador Kranzel*

Below:
*Tcherkasser William Kremer Lodge, founded in 1912
Philadelphia Jewish Archives Center at The Balch Institute. Gift of Esther
Weinberg*

In addition to the chevras, independent societies whose names often include such terms as "Young Men's" or "Progressive" sprang forth. There also was a proliferation of women's sections operating as auxiliaries to the male-dominated farein or as ladies aid societies engaged separately in social and charitable activities. Among others, we can point to the work of Philadelphia's Independent Kishineff Ladies Aid Society, the Pannonia Ladies Auxiliary, the Zitomirer Ladies Auxiliary, and the Zashkover Ladies Auxiliary of the Zashkover Unterstitzungs Farein. Other manifestations of affiliation with the town or city of origin are the relief organizations that sent aid to the native communities, particularly during pogroms and wartime. Family circles and cousins' clubs also adopted the organizational structure of the farein but were identified with either the ancestral name or that of a distinguished individual family member.

Above:
Membership brochure of the Samuel I. Vogelson Lodge No. 399, Brith Sholem (Checklist #77)

Left:
Roll Book of the Max Schermer Lodge No. 3, Independent Order Brith Sholem (Checklist #68)

Some landsmanshaftn chose to ally themselves
as branches of national Jewish orders, such as the
Tcherkasser William Kremer Lodge, the Samuel I.
Vogelson Lodge No. 399, or the Max Schermer
Lodge No. 3 of the Independent Order Brith Sholom. The meticulously preserved roll book of this
latter group serves as a useful census of candi-
dates who applied for membership between 1900
and 1921. For each name a page of background
data lists residence, age, occupation, marital status, and birthplace.

Below:
Women in the Workmen's Circle, from Forty Years Workmen's Circle, *1940
Balch Library Collection. Workmen's Circle (Philadelphia District) Papers*

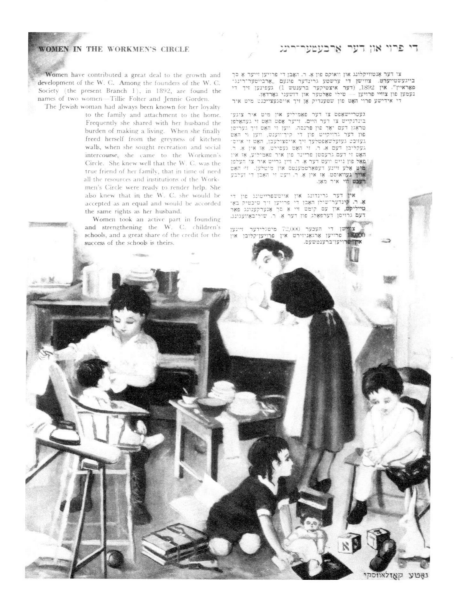

WOMEN IN THE WORKMEN'S CIRCLE

Women have contributed a great deal to the growth and
development of the W. C. Among the founders of the W. C.
Society (the present Branch 1), in 1892, are found the
names of two women—Tillie Folter and Jennie Gorden.

The Jewish woman had always been known for her loyalty
to the family and attachment to the home.
Frequently she shared with her husband the
burden of making a living. When she finally
freed herself from the greyness of kitchen
walls, when she sought recreation and social
intercourse, she came to the Workmen's
Circle. She knew well that the W. C. was the
true friend of her family, that in time of need
all the resources and institutions of the Workmen's Circle were ready to render help. She
also knew that in the W. C. she would be
accepted as an equal and would be accorded
the same rights as her husband.

Women took an active part in founding
and strengthening the W. C. children's
schools, and a great share of the credit for the
success of the schools is theirs.

די פרוי אין דער אַרבעטער־רינג

FARBAND *Labor Zionist Order*

פערציק יאריקער יוביליי

אלעסטער פראגרעסיוו בראנטש 301

Right:
Officers of Odesser Progressive Branch #301, Farband Labor Zionist Order,
from Fortieth Jubilee Book, 1913-1953 .
Philadelphia Jewish Archives Center at The Balch Institute. Gift of Labor Zionist Alliance

Below:
Workmen's Circle, Branch 575 (Checklist #284)

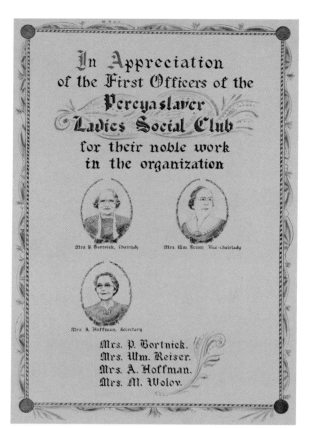

Some national parent organizations such as the Workmen's Circle, the Farband Jewish National Workers Alliance, and the International Workers Order attracted champions of distinct political viewpoints. The Workmen's Circle, for instance, held up its serious purpose of progressively defending workers' rights as an alternative to the initiation ceremonies and secret passwords of other Jewish lodges. In Philadelphia, among the local chapters of the Workmen's Circle that numbered at least ten before World War II, several carried place names such as Bialystoker or Rovner.[15] The Farband, a Zionist-oriented order, was similarly comprised of numerous landsmanshaft branches, including Anshe Zitomir Branch 2, Voliner Branch 3, Odesser Progressive Branch 301, Konover Branch 391, Pereyaslever Branch 318, and Ladies Odesser Branch 380.

Left:
First Officers of the Pereyaslaver Ladies Social Club, from Golden Book, Pereyaslaver Progressive Beneficial Association (Checklist #73)

Below:
Odesser Independent Beneficial Association membership certificate, early 20th c.
Balch Library Collection. Library Purchase

The intensity of landsmanshaft activity peaked in the early years of this century, with organizations burgeoning during World War I, when they actively helped finance relief work in their respective birthplaces in Europe. In a survey I conducted in the Philadelphia City Archives of requests for incorporation between the years 1900 and 1920, no fewer than sixty-five societies were identifiable by name as a landsmanshaft or farein.

The certificate of incorporation of the Independent Salchover Sick Beneficial Association of Philadelphia from 1913 is a prototype. Typically, names and addresses of officers and charter members are provided, and the mission of the group is clarified, in this case "to encourage among its members a fraternal spirit, to accumulate a fund of monthly dues which is to be applied to granting sick and death benefits in case of the sickness or death of any member."[16]

Above:
First Convention of all Berezovker Relief Societies in America and Canada (Checklist #76)

Below:
Krivozer Hilfs Farband Beneficial Association (Checklist #74)

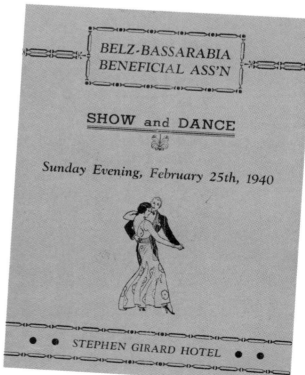

Left:
Testimonial to David Landis (Checklist #78)

Below:
Show and Dance program, Belz-Bessarabia Beneficial Association
(Checklist #81)

Besides assistance with the expenses related to burial, members of landsmanshaftn usually are assured allocation of gravesites and a proper Jewish funeral. When other elements of organizational activity have dwindled, this charge remains a prime concern. As a result, Jewish cemeteries and undertakers can be another source of information on landsmanshaft organizations in the city.

For valuable historical perspectives on Jewish organizational dynamics in Philadelphia, Moses Freeman's *Fuftsik yor geshikhte fun yidishn lebn in filadelfye* [Fifty Years of Jewish Life in Philadelphia] and Y. L. Malamut's *Filadelfyer yidishe anshtaltn un zeyere firer* [Philadelphia Jewish Institutions and their Leaders] are indispensable guides, and each devotes a sizable portion of the book to landsmanshaft associations. Further information can be gleaned from the files of major Jewish philanthropic and fundraising agencies, such as Israel Bonds, the Jewish National Fund, or the Israel Histadrut Campaign. Because they solicit funds from a variety of Jewish lodges, these offices compile directories of local groups. In 1948 the Allied Jewish Appeal enumerated well over one hundred benevolent societies and family circles in Philadelphia.[17] In this roster the penchant for creating multiple organizations to represent the same town is evident. We find, for example, Haisiner Beneficial Association and Haisiner Independent Young Men's Beneficial Association, Elisavetgrad Beneficial Association and Elisavetgrad Mutual Aid, Tolner Progressive Society and Tolner Dubner Brotherhood Association.

Particularly during World War I and World War II landsmanshaftn were prominent in coordinating fundraising efforts on a regional basis. As a result, coalitions such as the Mozirer and Vicinity Relief Committee functioned first from 1916 to 1929, and again from 1945 to 1952.[18] Once the crises pass, cooperation is not as likely to continue as many of these relief federations have disbanded. On the other hand, mergers have facilitated collaboration among several smaller groups. The United Jewish Organizations subsumes the former Brith Achim Beneficial Association, Elizabethgrad Beneficial Association, Smiler Unterstitzungs Verein, Zwengorodker Beneficial Association, and Kalisher-Stavistisher Beneficial Association. Another umbrella organization is the Boslover Ahavas Achim Belzer Association, which since 1952 has been comprised of the Boslover Beneficial Association, the Ahavas Achim Beneficial Association, and The Belz-Bessarabier Beneficial Association.

As the needs and circumstances of immigrant Jews and their American-born offspring are altered, the landsmanshaft recasts its original framework. One tendency has been for membership to cease being delimited solely by geography. Thus in 1909 the Young Roumanian Beneficial Association opened its doors to all, not only to those originating from the country which the title of the organization implies. In 1911 the Boslover Beneficial Association considered a motion that members be permitted to attend meetings without wearing a yarmulke or head cover, another sign of changing times. The same association eventually relocated from the Boslover Building at 7th and Pine, which served as headquarters for the twice monthly meetings convened by many societies, to Northeast Philadelphia.

Above:
Officers, Kaharliker Beneficial Association (Checklist #79)

The principal language of communication at meetings and in publications was Yiddish, destined to be replaced gradually by English. This pattern is apparent when comparing various updated editions of landsmanshaft constitutions or judging the span of an organization's correspondence. The record book of the Karhaliker Beneficial Association epitomizes the trend, with an unceremonious shift in 1952 from Yiddish script to Latin letters and a brief announcement to explain that future minutes will be kept in English.

Even as responses to issues and events are tempered by new situations, what remains at the core of all groups are the prescripts of mutual aid, the principles of social fellowship, and the central tenet of philanthropy. Standards for giving may change; still the rule is to donate to numerous causes. The Vitebsker Beneficial Association offers a model of how contributions have been granted: in support of the Federation of Jewish Charities in the city, to local workers in need, with funds to the Denver Consumptive Sanatorium, Denver National Jewish Hospital, and the Los Angeles Sanatorium, and donations of relief and packages to Palestine and to Vitebsk.

Since World War II concern for the native country understandably has been largely abandoned except as a focus of commemoration. The Wolkowysker and Vicinity Farein did not even form until 1945. Attempts to organize it failed until they were prompted by an appeal to aid those who had survived and to memorialize the annihilation of Wolkowysk. In this quest the organizers corresponded with counterparts in Israel and Argentina regarding their interest in publishing a *yisker* (memorial) book to document the achievements of Wolkowysk, as well as how it was destroyed by the Nazis. Over four hundred such memorial volumes have to date been sponsored and issued by individual societies throughout the world. Because their format is to reconstruct the history of the hometown and to summarize achievements of landsmanshaftn in different communities, the memorial books often include details about Philadelphia groups.

As landsmanshaft members learned of the destruction of European Jewry and witnessed the rise of the State of Israel, they shifted their focus from the old hometown to the new homeland. They joined various campaigns on behalf of Israel and also worked to locate and assist family and friends who had survived the Holocaust. This new configuration of landsmanshaft orientations is typified in a meeting notice from September 1948 of the United Brahiner and Vicinity Relief Committee of Philadelphia. Written in Yiddish, it urges members to attend an upcoming session to help decide:

> 1) should we help the Jews in Israel? 2) should we also help our landslayt in the old home, and if so, how? 3) should we join the central relief organization or should our relief efforts be conducted independently?[19]

The post-World War II refugees infused the landsmanshaft community with new spirit and new purpose. Some survivors joined existing societies in the city while others launched their own organizations such as the Association of Jewish New Americans, to give expression to their unique bond. Not surprisingly, the newcomers found, the previous waves of Jewish immigrants were comparatively distanced from the European hometown.

Even in the formative years of associational life in Philadelphia at the turn of the century, when immigrants had only recently arrived in the city from their native Russia or Poland, the process of disengagement was powerfully symbolized in the struggles to determine a name for their organizations. The establishment of the Vitebsker society was delayed because a vocal faction insisted on a name devoid of any reference to the birthplace of its members. Their proposal to identify the group only as the International Benevolent Association failed, but it reflects a paradoxical yet inevitable development, that the landsmanshaftn offered members a context in which to learn to become American.

The landsmanshaft sector in Philadelphia has been reduced in size, and the profile of its leadership has changed. Many societies have disbanded because their membership declined when the flow of immigrants subsided. Yet, contrary to all predictions, the landsmanshaftn did not disappear completely with the second and third American-born generations as children of pioneering founders were drawn into the ranks of leadership. And, there are signs of landsmanshaft continuity even into the 1980s.

Above:
Prushin-Shershow Lodge No. 132 (Checklist #72)

The Prushin-Shershow Beneficial Association will soon celebrate its centennial and is still vibrant. The *Jewish Exponent* periodically publishes photographs with descriptive captions to honor societies which work on behalf of Israel. The spirit of fellowship found in the farein has been borrowed and transformed by the Philadelphia Sons and Daughters of Jewish Holocaust Survivors. All of these signs give meaning to the observations of one current lodge leader, the son of a prominent landsmanshaft activist. When asked to account for the organizational durability and intergenerational continuity to which his own experience attests, his remark is instinctive and genuine: "Somebody has to carry on the traditions."[20]

In Philadelphia, eastern European Jews organized society after society to help them in their adjustment to their new home away from home. The farein helped the Jewish immigrant cope with life here and, in turn, the future of the association was destined to be shaped by the immigrant's accommodation to Philadelphia.

For members, the farein provides a forum in which to explore the changing meaning of their ethnicity. Until now the contribution of thousands of eastern European Jews who spontaneously created and participated in a multitude of immigrant associations has not been amply explored — all too often "their views were shared privately with a landsman over a glass of tea."[21] With materials now available and more that will be forthcoming, however, it is possible to raise that proverbial *glezele tey* and discover the inner world of Jewish associational life in the City of Brotherly (and Sisterly) Love.

Hannah Kliger *is Assistant Professor in the Department of Judaic and Near Eastern Studies and the Department of Communication at the University of Massachusetts (Amherst). Her two forthcoming books are:* Landslayt: A Retrospective Rediscovery *(Indiana University Press) and* Home Away From Home: Jewish Immigrant Associations in the United States and Israel *(Wayne State University).*

Above:
Beneficial society emblem from 25th Anniversary Banquet program, Zashkover Ladies' Auxiliary

Notes

1. Community surveys conducted in New York produced divergent counts of mutual aid societies in the city, some as high as 10,000. See, for example, the New York Kehilla's *Jewish Communal Register of New York City 1917-1918* (New York: Lipshitz Press, 1918); *List of Members of Jewish Communal Institutions in New York* (New York: Council of Jewish Communal Institutions, 1914); Federal Writers Project, *Di yidishe landsmanshaftn fun nyu york* [The Jewish Landsmanshaftn of New York] (New York: Yiddish Writers Union, 1938).

2. Rudolph J. Vecoli. "Diamonds in your own Backyard: Developing Documentation on European Immigrants to North American," *Ethnic Forum*, (September, 1981): 2-16.

3. Krakauer Beth Elohim Beneficial Society, One Hundredth Anniversary Journal [Philadelphia Jewish Archives Center at the Balch Institute (PJACBI) SC 82, May 15, 1976], 12. I have retained the spelling of organizational and place names as they appear in the records I discuss. Any translations from the Yiddish are my own.

4. David Sulzberger, "The Beginnings of the Russo-Jewish Immigration to Philadelphia," *Publications of the American Jewish Historical Society*, No. 19 (1910): 147.

5. Maxwell Whiteman, "The East European Jew Comes to Philadelphia," in *The Ethnic Experience in Pennsylvania*, ed. John E. Bodnar (Lewisburg, PA.: Bucknell University Press, 1971), 303-304.

43

6. *Jews of Philadelphia* (Records of the Works Progress Administration Pennsylvania Historical Survey, Ethnic Survey of Pennsylvania, 1938-39, unpublished manuscript), 135.

7. A copy of Volume I (June 5, 1919) of the *Jewish Advancer* is found in the files of the Chevra Bikur Cholim (PJACBI, ACC 1459). For a summary of periodicals that served the immigrant community, see also Dov Ber Tirkel, "Bibliografye fun der yidisher prese in filadelfye" [Bibliography of the Yiddish Press in Philadelphia], *Pinkes*, 1 (1927-28): 260-262.

8. Krakauer Beth Elohim Beneficial Society, *One Hundredth Anniversary*, 12.

9. *Ibid.*, 12.

10. *Ibid.*, 13.

11. Krakauer Beth Elohim Beneficial Society, *Constitution and By-Laws* (PJACBI, SC 82, 1929).

12. I. Shmulewitz, ed. *The Bialystoker Memorial Book.* (New York: Bialystoker Center, 1982).

13. See Federal Writers Project, *Di yidishe landsmanshaftn;* I. E. Rontch, "The Present State of the Landsmanshaften, " *Jewish Social Service Quarterly*, 15 (June 1939): 360-378; Hannah Kliger, "Traditions of Grass-Roots Organization and Leadership: The Continuity of Landsmanshaftn in New York," *American Jewish History*, 76 (September 1986): 25-39.

14. Richard N. Juliani, "The Social Organization of Immigration: The Italians in Philadelphia" (Ph.D. diss., University of Pennsylvania, 1971), 172-173.

15. See Judith Felsten, *Register of the Records of Workmen's Circle, Philadelphia District, 1931-1968, Mss. Group 42.* (Philadelphia: Balch Institute for Ethnic Studies, 1982)

16. City Archives of Philadelphia, *Charters Index*. Vol. 46 (February 14, 1913): 488.

17. My thanks to Robert Tabak for sending me a copy of this directory and to the former executive director of the Israel Histadrut Campaign, David Rosenthal, who generously provided me with a selected list of landsmanshaftn in Philadelphia known to his office. In 1983 I conducted interviews with members of four of these societies. For further details, see Hannah Kliger, "Communication and Ethnic Community: The Case of Landsmanshaftn" (Ph.D. diss., University of Pennsylvania, 1985).

18. Mozirer and Vicinity Relief Committee (American Jewish Archives, Cincinnati, Box 1746; Box 1811)

19. United Brahiner and Vicinity Relief Committee of Philadelphia, (American Jewish Archives, Cincinnati, Box 1811).

20. Interview by author with Sydney Landes at Boslover Ahavas Achim Belzer, 14 September, 1983.

21. Maxwell Whiteman, "Western Impact on East European Jews: A Philadelphia Fragment," in *Immigrants and Religion in Urban America*, eds. Randall M. Miller and Thomas D. Marzik (Philadelphia: Temple University Press, 1977), 121.

Above:
*American and Zionist flags, from 25th Anniversary Banquet program,
Zashkover Ladies' Auxiliary*

Suggested Reading

Bernheimer, Charles S., ed. *The Russian Jew in the United States.* Philadelphia: John C. Winston Company, 1905.

Federal Writers Project. *Di yidishe landsmanshaftn fun nyu york* [The Jewish Landsmanshaftn of New York]. New York: Yiddish Writers Union, 1938.

Freeman, Moses. *Fuftsik yor geshikhte fun yidishn lebn in filadelfye.* [Fifty Years of Jewish Life in Philadelphia]. Philadelphia: Mid-City Press, 1929.

Kliger, Hannah. "A Home Away from Home: Participation in Jewish Immigrant Associations in America." In *Persistence and Flexibility: Anthropological Perspectives on the American Jewish Experience,* edited by Walter P. Zenner, 143-64. Albany: State University of New York Press, 1988.

Malamut, Y. L. *Filadelfyer yidishe anshtaltn un zeyere firer* [Philadelphia Jewish Institutions and their Leaders] Philadelphia, 1942-1943.

Rontch, I. E. "The Present State of the Landsmanshaften," *The Jewish Social Service Quarterly* 15 (June 1939): 360-78.

Whiteman, Maxwell. "The East European Jew Comes to Philadelphia." In *The Ethnic Experience in Pennsylvania,* edited by John E. Bodnar, 303-4. Lewisburg, PA.: Bucknell University Press, 1973.

_____. "Philadelphia's Jewish Neighborhoods." In *The Peoples of Philadelphia,* edited by Allen F. Davis and Mark H. Haller, 231-54. Philadelphia: Temple University Press, 1973.

_____. "Western Impact on East European Jews: A Philadelphia Fragment." In *Immigrants and Religion in Urban America,* edited by Randall M. Miller and Thomas D. Marzik, 117-37. Philadelphia: Temple University Press, 1977.

IT USED TO BE LIKE JERUSALEM:
South Philadelphia, Portal to the City and Enduring Jewish Community

RAKHMIEL PELTZ

Above:
Fourth and Fitzwater Streets, 1914
Philadelphia City Archives

RIVKE, WHO CAME TO AMERICA IN 1923 at the age of twelve, remembers the bustling Jewish life in South Philadelphia of that time. *"O se flig zan vi Dzheruzalem."* (Oh it used to be like Jerusalem.)[1] Shmuel-Arn was born in South Philadelphia more than seventy years ago and has lived there all his life. Currently the president of Conservative congregation Adath Shalom at Marshall and Ritner Streets (in years gone by, known as Beys Shmuel, or the *litvishe shul*), Shmuel-Arn does not feel it at all necessary to qualify his statement to a meeting of the Philadelphia Jewish Community Relations Council that "Judaism started in South Philadelphia." The distinct Jewish nature of the neighborhood looms high in the consciousness of the residents.

The largest settlement of eastern European Jews in Philadelphia during the period of mass immigration was in South Philadelphia, just below South Street. This area became home to Jews who settled close to the docks that welcomed their ships. Because its population was replenished by new arrivals through the 1920s, South Philadelphia continued to be a major Jewish neighborhood until midcentury even though the older immigrants started moving out to areas such as Logan, Parkside, Southwest Philadelphia, Strawberry Mansion, and Wynnefield in the early 1900s.

South Philadelphia's Jewish population, estimated at 55,000 in 1907, later reached 100,000. A Philadelphia Housing Association Survey reported a drop of 41 percent in the number of Jews between 1920 and 1930, but in 1930 South Philadelphia was still the most populous Philadelphia Jewish neighborhood, numbering close to 50,000 Jews. Various reports appraised the area's Jewish population at 35,000 in 1942, 15,000 in 1958, and 3-4,000 in 1980.[2] After World War II Jews continued to leave for other neighborhoods, including Mt. Airy, Overbrook Park, and especially the Northeast and often moved again to suburban communities in Pennsylvania and southern New Jersey. As a result, the Jewish population of South Philadelphia declined more rapidly than that of the neighborhood's other ethnic groups, yet the ironies of Jewish geographic mobility would have it that the five communities of secondary settlement that were spawned largely by Jewish South Philadelphia at the beginning of the century today contain fewer Jews than does South Philadelphia. It is important to remember that although Jewish South Philadelphia has undergone changes, in many ways it is a continuation of the community of primary immigration.

Jewish South Philadelphia, a neighborhood analogous to New York's Lower East Side, has received scant attention in both scholarly and popular reports. As the little that has been written has focused on the original community of one hundred years ago, I will attempt to describe the richness of Jewish life that evolved during succeeding years in Philadelphia's longstanding Jewish neighborhood.

Above:
Kater Street, 1910 (Checklist #144)

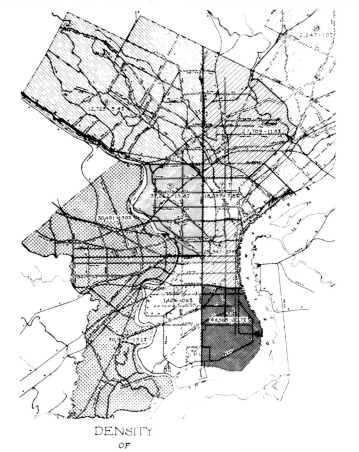

DENSITY
OF
GENERAL JEWISH POPULATION
1930

INDICATES THE NUMBER OF PUBLIC SCHOOL DISTRICT
INDICATES PROPORTION TO THE TOTAL JEWISH POPULATION
INDICATES SUBDIVISION OF 10 PUBLIC SCHOOL DISTRICTS

NOTE - BASED ON FEDERAL AND SCHOOL CENSUS

LEGEND

ASSOCIATED TALMUD TORAHS
OF PHILADELPHIA

Above:
*Density of General Jewish Population of Philadelphia,
1930, from* Jewish Education to the Fore, *Associated
Talmud Torahs of Philadelphia
Hebrew Union College*

Right:
*Residence and shop of Simon Mochrik, shoemaker,
508 S. 7th St., 1903
Urban Archives Center, Temple University*

The massive immigration of eastern European Jews to the United States commenced with the assassination of the Russian Tsar Alexander II in 1881 and the pogroms and repressive May Laws of 1882 which followed. The first ship carrying Russian Jewish immigrants that reached the Christian Street wharf arrived on February 23, 1882. In those early years most of the immigrants entering through the port did not stay in Philadelphia, but those who did remain quickly set up a Jewish community in the northeastern section of South Philadelphia, near South Street between Third and Sixth Streets. Although a small number of Jews had lived there earlier, by the time the new immigrants arrived, the area was known mainly as a slum and home to the underworld. Nevertheless, the place of immigrant residence during this period was most greatly influenced by proximity to employment. Consequently, South Philadelphia was a popular choice for the almost 40 percent of the immigrants employed in the garment industry and for the others working as peddlers or as keepers of stands and shops and in cigar factories.

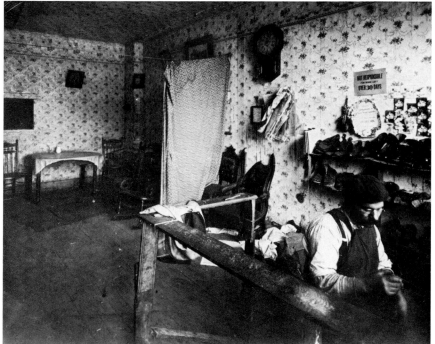

Above:
View of Fourth Street on market day (Checklist #263)

Right:
Strike broadside in English, Italian and Yiddish (Checklist #283)

Poor working conditions and the presence of Jewish anarchists and socialists very quickly made the community ripe for union organizing. Yiddish writer and journalist Moses Freeman operated a newsstand at Fifth and South and reported on the activities in full view at this infamous corner, known by the immigrants as the *khazer-mark* (hog market). Needle trade contractors and bosses could acquire Jewish immigrant labor here for a pittance. On weekday evenings and Sundays meeting rooms in the neighborhood were full of aggrieved Jewish workers intent on organizing unions. During the first major strike by Jewish clothing workers, for example, a mass meeting was organized by Cloakmakers Union No. 1 at Wheatley Hall, at Fifth and Gaskill Streets, on August 4, 1890, to protest the arrest of workers. Soon South Philadelphia would be dotted by the headquarters of workers' associations and unions with an overwhelmingly Jewish membership, such as the Bakers Union, the Philadelphia Men's and Kneepants Makers Union, the Vestmakers Union and the Agudes hashokhtim defiladelfya (Philadelphia Association of Ritual Slaughterers).[3]

SHIPLAKOFF Socialist Assembly man FROM NEW YORK STATE! IN PHILA.

The General Organizer of the A.C.W. of A. will speak in GARRICK HALL, Aug. 14th, 8 p.m.
FOR THE CUSTOM TAILORS OF PHILA.
COATS, PANTS and VESTS TAILORS come to this meeting you will learn a whole lot from our teacher, the Assembly man of New York.

FRATELLI E SORELLE

Voi tutti e tutte che lavorati collago per il vostro pezzo di pane quotidiano. Il tempo che dovete svegliarvi e giunto. Il tempo è giunto dovete organizzarvi in un forte e potente organizzazione di Sarti la quale vi strappera dalle dolorose condizioni, in una unione che voi ed it vostro mestiere dive formare la sua forza e la sua potenza, in una organizzazione che vi levera dalla presenti schiavitu, nella quale siete condannati nei secolo.

E necessario che vi ricordate delle condizioni di lavoro alle quali siete soggetti. Voi siete forzati a lavorare 16, 18 e 20 ore al giorno, e la Domenica fino alle 3 ed anche fino alle 4 p.m. e tornando di nuovo sul medesima lavoro, voi lavorate nei piu peggiori luoglei, dove non esistano condizioni sanitari. Negli alloggiamenti, in stanzette senza aria ed oscurissime, dietro il muro di qualche fabbricato o in qualche altro posto. La vostra paga e di $8 o $10 la settimana non piu.

Fratelli e Sorelle! Noi appelliamo e domandiamo a voi. Siete veramente soddisfatti di queste miserrime condizioni alle quale siete forgate a consumare tutte vostra vita? La risposta a questa domanda certamente deve essere: NO!!

Volete rompere le vostre catene di schiavitu?

Volete guadalmente la vostra vita?

Volete voi tutti tirare una vita piu comoda e piu felice per voi, per le vostre moglie ed i vostri figli?

Volete lavorare per nuno ore al giorno e piu moneta la settimana per il vostro duro lavoro?

La vostra risposte e arlamente: Si! Se cosi e, dunque vente da noi ed unitive alla Custom Tailors' Union che e gia organizzata, sotto la protezione della ricca e potente Amalgamated Clothing Workers of America.

Un Grande Comizio Internazionale

avra luogo

Sunedi 14 Agosto 1916, 8 p.m.
alla GARRICK HALL, 509 S. 8th Street

Ove parliranno i seguenti Oratori: Organizzatore Generale dell' A.C.W. of A.

S. SILVERMAN, parlera in ebraico.

In Italiano, **F. BELLANCO**, ed altri.

In questo comizio si discutera in dettagli le condizione di questo mestiere, e quale via si dovra battere per migliorare le nostre condizione.

District Council No. 2, of Phila., A.C.W. of A.

קאסטאם שנײדער ארבײטער!
קאום, װעסם, פענטס. באמעענהאל מיקערס און פענשערינס!

[Yiddish text column]

א גרויסער מאסס מיטינג

מאנטאג. אװנט דעם 14 טען סימן. 8. אחר אבענדס.
אין גערריק האל. 509 סיטה. 8. סטרית.

 אדיש. מ. סליווערמאן.
איטאליעניש פראנק בעלאנקא. און ערע־

[Yiddish text]

United Printing Company,   411 South Fifth Street

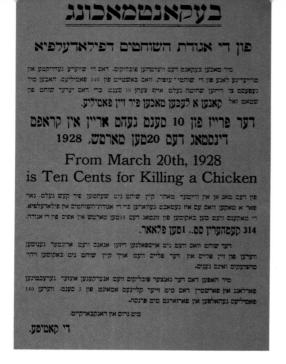

Above:
Kosher Slaughterers' notice of price increase (Checklist #272)

Still functioning, however, are three large synagogues established in the original immigrant quarter in the 1880s. The first Russian synagogue in Philadelphia, Bnai Abraham, was begun in 1882 and moved to its present location at Sixth and Lombard in 1885. In 1891, Rabbi Bernard Levinthal arrived in Philadelphia to serve the congregation and for the next sixty years he led Philadelphia's Orthodox Jewish life and was a figure of national prominence as well. Kesher Israel at Fourth and Lombard represents the union in 1894 of Bnai Jacob founded in 1883 and Rodfey Tsedek founded in 1887. The Roumanian American Congregation (Oir Chodash Agudath Achim), organized in 1886 at 512 S. 3rd Street, moved to Fourth and Spruce Streets in 1901, calling its synagogue *Di groyse rumeynishe shul* (The Great Roumanian Synagogue). Currently the congregation in known as the Society Hill Synagogue.

Below:
Roumanian American Synagogue, c. 1890
Society Hill Synagogue Collection

In many facets of life, South Philadelphia would house the citywide headquarters of Jewish organizations for many years to come. The proximity to Center City made the neighborhood a convenient locale for meetings. As organizational life developed in the city, South Philadelphia branches of organizations often acquired the designation Downtown as part of their name though South Philadelphians themselves use "in town" to refer to locations in the central part of the city.

The development of a diverse religious life accompanied the new immigration. On the same block that witnessed the mass cloakmakers' rally, the Hungarian Synagogue (Emunas Israel Ohev Sholom) had opened in 1888 in the former Garrick Theater. One of the founders pawned his gold watch in order to buy a Torah scroll for the new synagogue. In its heyday the shul had three weekday morning services plus three evening study groups, and on Saturdays several hundred people attended services. It closed in 1967.[4]

In 1905, Charles S. Bernheimer wrote that Jews were already moving to the more southern streets near Moore Street, but his list of nineteen local shuls does not contain any located that far south. It is certain that several years later a sizable number of Jewish institutions had opened their headquarters there. For example, nine branches of the Workmen's Circle formed a labor lyceum on Sixth and Tasker Streets in 1912. The Downtown Jewish Orphanage opened on the same street during the influenza epidemic after the first World War but moved further south to Ninth and Shunk in 1925. The two largest Orthodox shuls in the expanded region of secondary settlement in South Philadelphia were erected at Eighth and Porter and Fourth and Porter in 1912 and 1913, Shaari Eliohu and Shaari Israel. Several current residents remember that their families moved to the shopping street at Seventh *(di zibete)* near Porter during World War I, and the area was already mostly Jewish. It is exactly here that most Jewish residents of South Philadelphia are concentrated seventy-five years later.

Institutions sometimes experienced administrative and financial difficulties in relocating to an area close to their clientele. For example, the Neighborhood Center, an important settlement house for immigrants that remained a Jewish recreational and cultural center, did not move from Fifth and Bainbridge Streets to Marshall and Porter Streets until 1948. Reincorporated within the Federation of Jewish Charities in 1918, the Neighborhood Center was previously known as the Young Women's Union. It was one of the original Federation constituents in 1901 and had pioneered the first kindergarten, nursery school, day care center, and probationary supervision and foster homes for children of immigrants.[5] In 1900 the public schools near the settlement house had enrollments of 85-95 percent Jewish children and in 1948 only 10-15 percent.[6]

Above:
Neighborhood Day Nursery student in Russian costume (Checklist #95)

Left:
Jewish Educational Center #2 (currently the Stiffel Senior Center), 1983 Philadelphia Jewish Archives Center at The Balch Institute. Courtesy of L. Knight and R. Peltz.

Below:
Associated Talmud Torahs pupil record, from Jewish Education to the Fore Hebrew Union College

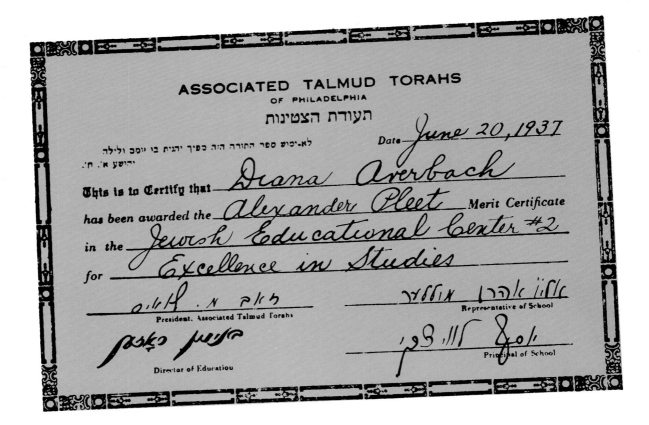

ASSOCIATED TALMUD TORAHS
OF PHILADELPHIA

תעודת הצטינות

לא-יכוש ספר התורה ה:ה כפ:ך יהגיח בי יסמכ וליל:ה
יהושע א'. ח'.

Date June 20, 1937

This is to Certify that *Diana Averbach*

has been awarded the *Alexander Pleet* Merit Certificate

in the *Jewish Educational Center #2*

for *Excellence in Studies*

President, Associated Talmud Torahs

Representative of School

Director of Education

Principal of School

In its new location the Neighborhood Center was to share the building of a modern Talmud Torah, which had opened its doors in 1928 as the Jewish Educational Center No. 2 (Center No. 1 was established at the same time at Fifth and Moore Streets).[7] The descendant of this institution is the current Stiffel Senior Center of the Jewish Community Centers of Philadelphia. Many of the Senior Center's current members attended the Talmud Torah more than fifty years ago in the same building. Their children studied at the Talmud Torah too, in addition to going there to day camp, religious services, teen dances, and basketball games. Beyle, for example, recalls teaching there as a teenager and having singer Eddie Fisher as one of her student cantors. In some cases the parents of today's members became the first members of the newly converted Senior Center fifteen years ago. Thus the life cycle of the institution has coincided with the personal and family life cycles of the Jews of South Philadelphia.

To counteract the influence of the Protestant Bethel Mission, which offered attractive recreational activities for youths in a heavily populated Jewish area, the Federation operated a Neighborhood House at Sixth and Mifflin Streets from 1922 until 1943, at the border between wards 1 and 39. Throughout its existence the Neighborhood House suffered from poor physical conditions and was supervised by the Neighborhood Center from 1930 to 1940. Nevertheless, in 1937 the Neighborhood House had over one thousand members; 95 percent were Jewish, 97 percent native-born, and 93 percent lived in row houses with restricted play spaces.[8]

Above:
Students at the Jewish Neighborhood House Progress School (Checklist #246 and #245)

During most of the period since the beginning of mass immigration South Philadelphia has been the hub of Jewish organizational, religious, and business life. A survey of four weeks of the Philadelphia Yiddish daily *Di yidishe velt* of April 1941 finds the meeting announcements of thirty-one different Jewish organizations in the neighborhood. A sampling serves to illustrate their diversity: mutual aid societies such as the Heysiner Independent Young Men's Association, United Ezras Akhim Ahaves Sholem Beneficial Association, Banos Sholem Free Loan Society, charitable groups which included the Downtown Froyen Lekhem Oniyem Fareyn and the South Philadelphia branch that raised money for the Philadelphia Psychiatric Hospital, branches of Zionist organizations such as Hadassah and Poaley-tsiyon, and the Anshey Zhitomir branch of the Jewish Nationalist Workers Alliance. Established by immigrants soon after they came to this country, these organizations would most often conduct their affairs in Yiddish. The participation of children of immigrants was not precluded, but for Jews and many other immigrant groups South Philadelphia continued to be the main home of those born in the old country.

Some of the principal Jewish social service agencies in Philadelphia continued to maintain their headquarters in the neighborhood. Besides the Neighborhood Center, also functioning in South Philadelphia as late as 1948 were the Jewish Welfare Society (a family casework agency), the Downtown Hebrew Day Nursery, a residence hotel for young Jewish working women, the Home for the Aged and Infirm Hebrews, the Downtown Hebrew Orphan Asylum, and Mt. Sinai Hospital.[9]

Left:
Outside Jewish Neighborhood House on trip to Overbrook School
(Checklist #99)

Right:
Synagogue B'nai Moishe, 5th and Watkins Sts., 1975
Photo by Marc Toplin
Philadelphia Jewish Archives Center at The Balch Institute.
Study of Ward I

Below:
Hevra Mategide Tehillum, 6th and Mercy Sts., 1975
Photo by Marc Toplin
Philadelphia Jewish Archives Center at The Balch Institute.
Study of Ward I

South Philadelphia was also the home of a myriad of synagogues and religious schools. Citywide registers for 1934 and 1943, a period when the neighborhood accounted for less than 15-20 percent of the city's Jewish population, locate one-third of Philadelphia's synagogues in the area.[10] At that time, the local synagogues were more traditional than those in any other neighborhood. Not only were they all Orthodox, but the names reflect the oldest kind of synagogue founded by eastern European immigrant Jews, the *anshey,* in which members hailed from the same hometown. One observer has commented that "South Philadelphia . . . once contained as many Jews as Italians (if not more), but the area shows no evidence of ever having been a Jewish ghetto, so complete was the out-migration."[11] This is, however, not true; the buildings that housed scores of synagogues and former Jewish institutions still stand as the most obvious reminders of the prevailing Jewish community of yesterday.

מאנילניצקי'ס פֿאלקס-שולע, 716 ס. 5טע סט.

Dear Mr_____   איך מאך אייך היערמיט

Your_____   אויפֿמערקזאם דאס אייער

was absent from School   _____ איז ניט געווען

on_____   אין סקוהל

Kindly see to it that_____   וואס איז די אורזאכע ?

returns to school to-day and attends   זעהט, אז_____ זאל פֿון

more regularly.   היינט אן אמענדען רעגעלמעסיג.

Yours truly,   עהרעבענסט,

JOSEPH MAGIL   יוסף מאגילניצקי,

Above:
School notice to parents regarding absenteeism (Checklist #248)

Home to a diverse assortment of institutions fostering the continuity of eastern European Jewish culture, South Philadelphia also included the adult branches and children's schools of organizations that advocated the perpetuation of Yiddish language and culture: the Workmen's Circle, the Jewish Nationalist Workers Alliance, and, until it fell victim to Senator McCarthy's crusade in the 1950s, the communist-leaning Jewish People's Fraternal Order of the International Workers Order.

The Jewish press today does not indicate that the prominent leaders of the city's Jewish community still reside in South Philadelphia even though the neighborhood can still boast of Jewish professionals and politicians. In contrast, a 1942-43 compendium of "eminent citizens and industrialists" includes no fewer than eleven South Philadelphia residents.[12]

In earlier times the Jewish nature of the neighborhood was conveyed as much by the diversity of stores that would spill over onto street stands as by the synagogues and institutions, doctors, and politicians. Jewish shopkeepers sold their wares throughout the area, but the concentrated shopping streets were Fourth Street *(di ferde)* in the north and the zibete in the south. Residents remember that in the 1940s there were four kosher butchers on a single block of the zibete. They recall with nostalgia the stores that were open past midnight, the *kvas* (cider) stand, and the peanut store with the pinball machines, as well as the Saturday promenades to socialize and show off your best and the flowing Yiddish speech, the language of commerce on the zibete and the ferde.

The residential area was dominated by two-story brick row houses. Leye remembers the new houses at Third and Gladstone Streets to which she moved with her family in 1912. This location still is home to South Philadelphia Jews today. Yisroel, a 96-year-old immigrant from Volhynia who worked as a carpenter, lived for seventy years on the street on which Leye settled initially. Khatshe, a 100-year-old immigrant baker, moved into his house in 1918, close to the only Orthodox shul that still functions, Shivtei Yeshuron-Heisiner-Ezras Israel, built in 1913. Roze was born at Fourth and Bainbridge Streets in the center of the original immigrant area and attended the Jewish Day Nursery and Neighborhood Center. When she was very young, she and her family moved further south and never left the neighborhood.

Above:
Durfor Street, Mifflin Square (Checklist #159)

Kelman has spent all of his years in South Philadelphia. Born in the more northern section of the neighborhood, he moved together with eight family members in 1924 to the building on the zibete that until recently housed his luncheonette. After graduating from Southern High, he worked at several occupations: running a fish and fruit store with his mother, owning a wholesale fruit business, selling life insurance, vending soft ice cream, and manufacturing and wholesaling his own water ice. For the forty-eight years since he married Sure, who came to America at age ten from Ukraine, Kelman has lived in a nicely furnished house with a front porch, a few blocks from his luncheonette, nearer to an Italian-American area. Here their son and daughter grew up. Kelman is more active than many men half his age. He is the main organizer of Y.P.C. Shari Eli synagogue, as well as his landsmanshaft. In addition, he has been an officer of the four different Masonic groups to which he belongs. The elderly residents of current South Philadelphia appreciate Kelman's concern, charity, and devotion to people and social groups. His gentle strength and influence pervade and help to define this Jewish community.

Feygl-Asye has lived in her house for forty-one years. But her previous three residences were all within one block of her present home. In this neighborhood she went to school, graduating from Southern High School for Girls and also completing the Talmud Torah in the present Senior Center. South Philadelphia residents view their neighborhood of today and of yesteryear as warm and friendly. Feygl-Asye recalls: "Here were *heymishe* (familiar) people who knew me and I knew them, and I liked them, and they me . . . I used to look at the whole neighborhood as I walked home, I liked it here, here were *mentshn* (real people); in other places *hot men gehot fley in de nuz* (people were stuck up) . . . Here were the best Jews in all of Philadelphia."

Below:
Apron salesman, 2nd and Fitzwater Sts. (Checklist #277)

Above:
Margulis Kosher wine shop, 2nd and Fitzwater Sts., 1938
Philadelphia Evening Bulletin/*Temple Urban Archives.*

Although South Philadelphia was changing and dynamic, it retained the image of the immigrant area, a place for up-and-coming young Americans to be ashamed of. The scorn and low prestige were communicated especially by residents who had moved to greener pastures. Tsipe-Khashe, who still lives in the neighborhood, remembers that in the 1930s South Philadelphia Jews were stigmatized as being poor, and her girlfriends were happy to move away because they feared otherwise they would not marry a boy from a proper background. In reaction those remaining evolved an attitude of fierce neighborhood pride.

The residential pattern of South Philadelphia consisted of ethnically homogeneous streets running in a north-south direction, with the Jews residing between Third and Eighth Streets, Italians to the west, and Irish and Polish immigrants to the east along the waterfront. Ethnic relations were far from peaceful; territory was often defended. Up through today, Jews have tended to enjoy better relations with their Italian-American neighbors than with other ethnic groups, and some intermarried with members of this group. By contrast, the most vivid memories of American-born Jewish residents are of the attacks by Irish-American children on the way to school.

The major way that South Philadelphia Jews identify with being Jewish is not now, nor has it ever been, synagogue attendance although many residents do attend synagogue. Instead they refer to yiddishkeit, an overall sense of being Jewish that has pervaded their existence since their youth. This state of being, as they define it, includes growing up with Jewish family and neighbors, believing in God, observing the dietary laws, preparing traditional dishes, speaking Yiddish, celebrating holidays, being interested in Jewish issues, and exhibiting strong ethnic pride. There is great variation in observance and sense of yiddishkeit among the current elderly residents who grew up in South Philadelphia, but the Jewish neighborhood life of their youth instilled in all of them confidence about their own adherence to Jewish ways.

60

Having stayed closer to the immigrant generation than most of their contemporaries, American-born residents of South Philadelphia have retained their Yiddish language. They report that they spoke Yiddish mainly with their parents but usually not with siblings. In Ester-Sosye's household speaking English at home was strictly prohibited, punishable by a slap in the face. Her parents were convinced that the only language of discourse befitting a Jewish household was Yiddish. Dveyre and Surele, who both came from England to South Philadelphia as infants, reported that although their parents spoke English well, they always spoke Yiddish with the children. Some of the best real-life stories told by these children of immigrants relate to their first day in school, having been born in the neighborhood, but not knowing English until their entry into the public schools.

Nostalgia runs strong in South Philadelphia. Several residents remember going with their mother or grandmother to Leybele *shprekher* (the exorcist) who could ward off the evil eye. Mothers would try to insure the health of sick children by giving them an additional name such as *Khaye* (life) or by employing the custom of buying back sick children from the devil. Rivke recalls that her mother put a knife under her pillow when she was giving birth so that the weapon would be *sheydik tse sheydim* (harmful to the evil spirits). Although the residents do not practice such folk beliefs now, they have trust in their powers and get vicarious pleasure by recalling times when these practices were used.

Residents of South Philadelphia report that their parents did not strictly observe Jewish religious laws. Most of them worked on shabbos, yet they knew when shabbos began and what it required. On the zibete after the shabbos candles were lit in the kitchen behind the store, the kitchen door was closed so that the shopkeeper would not have to walk past the candles while he was working. Beyle reports that her father, a baker, would work all of Friday night and go to shul early Saturday morning when he came home from work. Similarly, Robert Lasson remembers that he would work in his uncle's woolens store on the ferde while his uncle attended shul on Saturday, the big day for the business.[13] The South Philadelphia Jews are traditional, albeit selective in the traditions they observe.

South Philadelphia's Jewish community today is miniscule when compared with its predecessor at the turn of the century. Nevertheless, the innovative dedication of the "young people's congregations," which started in South Philadelphia in the 1930s and 1940s, the flurry of activities at the Jewish War Veterans Post and Ladies Auxiliary and at the local Jewish Masonic Square Club, and the day-to-day vibrancy of the Senior Center all speak to the continuity of an intense Jewish neighborhood tradition. For over one hundred years, South Philadelphia has inspired Jewish life throughout the city.

Left:
Mr. and Mrs. Leybele Satanoffsky and family (Checklist #129)

Rakhmiel Peltz *has a Ph.D. in cellular biology (University of Pennsylvania) and in Yiddish Studies (Columbia University). He is a Research Associate at the YIVO Institute for Jewish Research and teaches at Boston University. He is completing a book on Yiddish language and Jewish identity in South Philadelphia.*

Notes

1. The Yiddish first names used in the text refer to South Philadelphia residents with whom the author conversed during his field work (1982-1985). Many of the quotations are translations from Yiddish by the author. Jerusalem in this quotation should not be confused with the appellation for an earlier small settlement of eastern European Jews in the northern Port Richmond section. In this article, English words originating from Yiddish and Hebrew are not indicated by italics if they are included in *Webster's Third New International Dictionary of the English Language Unabridged* (Springfield, MA.: E. and C. Merriam Company, 1981).

2. Charles S. Bernheimer, ed., *The Russian Jew in the United States* (Philadelphia: John C. Winston Co., 1905), 51-2; Maxwell Whiteman, "Philadelphia's Jewish Neighborhoods," in *The Peoples of Philadelphia,* eds. Allen F. Davis and Mark H. Haller (Philadelphia: Temple University Press, 1973), 246; Richard A. Varbero, "Philadelphia's South Italians in the 1920s," *ibid.,* 261; Ben Rosen, ed., *Jewish Education to the Fore* (Philadelphia: Associated Talmud Torahs of Philadelphia, 1938); Julian L. Greifer, "Neighborhood Center — A Study of the Adjustment of a Cultural Group in America," (Ph.D. diss., New York University, 1948), 487; Julian L. Greifer, MS in Neighborhood Center collection, Philadelphia Jewish Archives Center at the Balch Institute (PJACBI) MSS 10/3, Box 1, Folder 1. Draft of address to the tenth anniversary celebration of the Neighborhood Center South, 1958, p. 5; Norma Rotman, *Health Needs Assessment and Social History of the Jewish Population of South Philadelphia* (Philadelphia: Albert Einstein Medical Center Daroff Division, 1980), 7.

3. Moses Freeman, *Fuftsik yor geshikhte fun yidishn lebn in filadelfye* (Philadelphia: Mid-city Press, 1929), 72, 63, 65; Maxwell Whiteman, "Western Impact on East European Jews: A Philadelphia Fragment," in *Immigrants and Religion in Urban America,* eds. Randall M. Miller and Thomas D. Marzik (Philadelphia: Temple University Press, 1977), 122-35.

4. Harry Beitchman, MS in PJACBI, Accessions 120 and 123, "History of the Hungarian Synagogue — Chevra Emunas Israel Ohev Sholom," (c. 1967), 1, 4-5.

5. Philip Rosen, "German Jews vs. Russian Jews in Philadelphia Philanthropy," in *Jewish Life in Philadelphia: 1830-1940,* ed. Murray Friedman (Philadelphia: ISHI Publications, 1983), 200-01.

6. Greifer, "Neighborhood Center," 144, 264-66.

7. Ben Rosen, *Jewish Education.*

8. Greifer, "Neighborhood Center," 267-71.

9. *Ibid.,* 335.

10. *Seyfer Hazikorin: Souvenir Journal Commemorating the Celebration of the Fortieth Anniversary of the Yeshiva Mishkan Israel and Central Talmud Torah* (Philadelphia: 1934), 45-47; Y. L. Malamut, *Filadelfyer yidishe anshtaltn un zeyere firer* (Philadelphia: 1942-43), 286-289.

11. Caroline Golab, *Immigrant Destinations* (Philadelphia: Temple University Press, 1977), 165.

12. Malamut, 109-74.

13. Robert Lasson, "It's Fourth St. — of another time," *Jewish Exponent,* 24 February 1984, 48-49.

Suggested Reading

Bernheimer, Charles S., ed. *The Russian Jew in the United States.* Philadelphia: John C. Winston Company, 1905.

Freeman, Moses. *Fuftsik yor geshikhte fun yidishn lebn in filadelfye.* Philadelphia: Mid-city Press, 1929.

Golab, Caroline. *Immigrant Destinations.* Philadelphia: Temple University Press, 1977.

Lasson, Robert, "It's Fourth St. — of another time." *Jewish Exponent,* 24 February 1984, 48-49.

Malamut, Y. L. *Filadelfyer yidishe anshtaltn un zeyere firer.* Philadelphia, 1942-43.

Miller, Fredric M., Morris J. Vogel and Allen F. Davis. *Still Philadelphia: A Photographic History,* 1890-1940. Philadelphia: Temple University Press, 1983.

Peltz, Rakhmiel. "Who's Speaking Yiddish in South Philadelphia Today? Jewish Language in Urban America." *International Journal of the Sociology of Language* 67 (1987): 145-66.

Tabak, Robert. "Orthodox Judaism in Transition." In *Jewish Life in Philadelphia 1830-1940,* edited by Murray Friedman, 48-63. Philadelphia: ISHI Publications, 1983.

Whiteman, Maxwell. "Philadelphia's Jewish Neighborhoods." In *The Peoples of Philadelphia,* edited by Allen F. Davis and Mark H. Haller, 231-54. Philadelphia: Temple University Press, 1973.

_____. "Western Impact on East European Jews: A Philadelphia Fragment." In *Immigrants and Religion in Urban America,* edited by Randall M. Miller and Thomas D. Marzik, 117-37. Philadelphia: Temple University Press, 1977.

REFLECTIONS OF THE COMMUNITY:
Through the Eyes of Jewish Photographers

ELIZABETH HOLLAND

LIKE PASSPORTS, NATURALIZATION PAPERS, birth and death certificates, marriage licenses, and other documents, photographs can be a valuable resource for family and community history. From them we can learn about relationships, family life, clothing trends, portrait trends, rituals, celebrations, rites of passage, and community and national events. Photographs permanently freeze a moment in time on a two-dimensional surface. As picture makers working with chemicals, light, and images, photographers are artists, event recorders, portrait makers, and sometimes inventors and innovators. Many of Philadelphia's Jewish photographers have made lasting contributions by documenting the life of the city's Jewish community. This essay will examine a representative sampling of their work; there are far more photographers than the limited number that can be treated here.

Below:
Self-portrait, c. 1865
Photograph by Levy and Solis-Cohen
Library Company of Philadelphia

Commercial Photography

PHOTOGRAPHERS PRODUCE IMAGES for both public and private consumption. Photojournalists and documentary photographers traditionally have created images for publication or mass production. As early as 1865, the Philadelphia photographic team of **Cornelius Levy** (?-1865) and **Leon Solis-Cohen** (1840-1884) documented the aftermath of the Civil War with their "Views in and Around Richmond." In their studios at Ninth and Filbert Streets they followed the example of Matthew Brady and other Civil War photographers, who made documentary images available to those collecting "mementoes of the war," producing cartes de visite and "whole size" images of "all the points of historical interest in and about" the Rebel capital. This use of photographic images opened a new world of reporting and recording. As the *Philadelphia Photographer* stated in 1865, "No pen is required" to describe the "ruin and desolation" of the city of Richmond.[1]

Louis Edward Levy (1846-1919), a photochemist and inventor, foresaw the advantages of using photographic images to accompany news stories. Born in Stenowitz, Bohemia, he emigrated with his parents to the United States and settled with them in Detroit when he was nine years old. He invented a practical photoengraving process known as the "Levytype" while working with David Bachrach in Baltimore, and in 1875 he moved to Philadelphia where he established the Levytype Company with his brother Max. Working together, the brothers developed a number of photographic processes for which they received invention and science awards. Later they incorporated a publishing department into the business when Louis Levy bought two newspapers, the *Evening Herald* and *The Mercury: An Illustrated Sunday Newspaper*. Here Louis put into production the illustrating methods he had developed. An author as well as a pioneer in the field of photoengraving, Louis Levy compiled *The Jewish Year* (1895), *The Jewish Refugees in the United States* (1895), and *Recollections of Forty Years: A Photo-Engraving Retrospective* (1912). As one of the founders and the second president of the Association for the Protection of Jewish Immigrants, he was also a prominent Philadelphia civic leader.[2]

Above:
Memorial Meeting program for Louis Edward Levy, under the auspices of the Jewish Community in Philadelphia, 23 March, 1919 (detail)
Maxwell Whitman Collection

Left:
"Views in and Around Richmond," 1865: Libby Prison
Carte de visite by Levy and Solis-Cohen
Library Company of Philadelphia

Above:
"A Typical Scene in the Russian Jewish Quarter of Philadelphia,"
Levytype photoengraving.
Photograph by D.F. Rowe.
Maxwell Whiteman Collection

Levytypes were an early, successful attempt at producing photographic
half-tones for reproduction.

Right:
The Mercury: An Illustrated Sunday Newspaper, *1889*
Maxwell Whiteman Collection

Levytype photoengravings were used as illustrations for The Mercury.

HENRY M. STANLEY.

Jacob Stelman (1905-1974) was born in Warren, Pennsylvania, of Russian Jewish immigrants and taught himself photography after many years in the printing business. At about age sixteen he began working as a "printer's devil" (sweeping and running errands) in a printing shop where he learned the trade by observing the printers who worked there. He later found a printing job at Franklin Printing in Philadelphia and while working there in the early 1930s began experimenting with photography. In 1936 he opened a studio for commercial photography in the city.[3]

Above:
Self-portrait, 1956
Photograph by Jacob Stelman
Courtesy of Harriet Joyce Epstein

Right:
Franklin and Eleanor Roosevelt, Senator Joseph F. Guffey, and John B.
Kelly on their way to Convention Hall to attend the Bicentennial
Celebration of the University of Pennsylvania, 1940.
Photograph by Jacob Stelman
Courtesy of Harriet Joyce Epstein

Below:
Annual Picnic of the Beth Israel Religious School, c. 1940
Photograph by Jacob Stelman
Courtesy of Harriet Joyce Epstein

Studio Photography

PACKING UP A FEW of their most valuable possessions, large numbers of eastern European Jews fled poverty and political persecution in their homelands and came to the United States during the late nineteenth and early twentieth centuries. By 1900 more than 30,000 Russian Jews lived in Philadelphia and that number more than tripled over the next two decades. Coming to a new country meant change—a new way of life, new jobs and careers, and for many, raising a family in new surroundings. One means of maintaining the family's heritage and the traditions of the homeland was the preservation of family photographs. Photos were almost always among the limited possessions Jewish immigrants brought with them on their journey, for the pictures provided a visual history and reminder, triggering the mind with memories and stories. Photographs also were considered important to send to relatives and friends in the homeland and conveyed information on how the immigrants fared in America. For this reason, most studio photographers offered 4" x 6" postcards as well as 5" x 7" and 8" x 10" prints.

As an artist, the photographer was responsible for presenting to his client a personal likeness. This likeness was generally expected to be a positive image and often was taken on the occasion of a rite of passage, such as a Bar Mitzvah or wedding, or in conjunction with another happy event. The sitter arrived in the studio well dressed and usually posed, often against a studio backdrop. Later, negative retouchers used a fine pencil to fill in wrinkle lines, cover up blemishes, and solidify any of the blurring that often occurred. In this way, clients could provide their families at home with an image of life in America that was happy, prosperous, and virtually flawless.

Below:
B. Mednik business card, c. 1914
Courtesy of Clare Lewin and Seymour Mednick

1611 So. 8th Street

B. Mednik
ARTIST
Specialist in Portraiture Painting
in Oil and Water Color
Pastil Crayon and Sepia
Philadelphia, Pa

Studio photographers produced photographs for a personal, private audience. Such photos had value and meaning only for those who were familiar with the subjects. Jewish photographers who specialized in portrait work in Philadelphia during the early years of the twentieth century included Max Pomerantz, Osias Goldstein, Charles Osias Haimovitz, Daniel Slutsky, Elias Goldensky, and Benjamin Mednick. Some of these men worked in South Philadelphia where the majority of new arrivals from eastern Europe settled. Having come to a strange land, immigrants sought comfort in familiarity. Most Jewish businessmen in this area, including photographers, spoke Yiddish and attracted a clientele which shared this common language. Other photographers served the Jewish community located north of Market Street, between Spring Garden and Diamond, and from Front Street to 17th Street. The work of both included individual and family portraits commemorating Bar Mitzvahs, birthdays, and weddings, as well as community portraits such shul classes and organizational banquets.

Above:
Mednick Family (Clockwise: Benjamin, Bessie, Sol, Seymour and Clare), 1933
Photograph by Benjamin Mednick
Courtesy of Clare Lewin and Seymour Mednick

As a student at the Academia en Odessa, Mednick was trained to create harmony and balance in his still life compositions. He treated his photographic subjects in the same way.

Left:
Benjamin and Clare, 1923
Photograph by Benjamin Mednick
Courtesy of Clare Lewin and Seymour Mednick

Benjamin Mednick (1893-1945) served primarily a family-oriented clientele. Born Borris Mednitzky in Kishinev, Russia, he attended the Academia en Odessa where he studied fine arts. In the summer of 1914 he sailed for America from Bremen, Germany, on the vessel *Friedrich Der Grosse* in order to avoid conscription into the Russian Army.

Left:
Clare's Halloween Party, 1926
Photograph by Benjamin Mednick
Courtesy of Clare Lewin and Seymour
Mednick

Below:
Seymour's Birthday Party, 1932
Photograph by Benjamin Mednick
Courtesy of Clare Lewin and Seymour
Mednick

Right:
Hymie Prizant with his niece Mildred, 1920
by Benjamin Mednick
Courtesy of Clare Lewin and Seymour
Mednick

Below:
Class of the I. L. Peretz School under the
sponsorship of the Workmen's Circle,
1930-31
Photograph by Benjamin Mednick
Courtesy of Clare Lewin and Seymour
Mednick

I. L. Peretz Schools under the sponsorship of
the Workmen's Circle were established in
1918 to cultivate in the children of members
an "understanding of the civic and social
problems confronting" Jewish Americans.

Above:
Max Bass, Abe Prizant, Benjamin Mednick, and Joe Prizant, 1915
Photographic postcard by Samuel Sax
Courtesy of Clare Lewin and Seymour Mednick

The Yiddish Theater was an important recreational activity for many Jewish immigrants. Mednick's cousin and close friend Hymie Prizant wrote music and acted in the theater. In Mednick's studio, Prizant and his friends acted out scenes from plays they had seen, or created their own dramatic situations and photographed them.

After settling in Philadelphia Mednitzky changed his name to Benjamin Mednik and established himself as an artist who specialized in portrait painting at 1611 S. 8th Street. Eventually he again changed the spelling of his name to "Mednick." He married Bessie Lerman in about 1918 and they had three children. Discovering that photography was quicker and less expensive than painted portraiture, Mednick readily found work in the studios of several photographers. For White's (4th and South Streets), Sinkov's (1835 S. 7th Street), and Roma's (800-802 Christian Street) studios, he hand-tinted photographs and retouched negatives. In 1920 he established a studio which often doubled as a dining hall and secret meeting place for unions in his home at 1809 North 31st Street, and enlisted each member of his family in the production of photographs. Two of his children, Clare Lewin and Seymour Mednick, recall that their Mondays were devoted to developing the negatives of the weekend's sittings; Tuesdays were for initial retouching and making proofs; Wednesdays were for coloring; Thursdays were for final retouching and starting to print; and Fridays were for printing. Saturdays were for finishing, mounting, framing and getting orders ready for delivery to customers. In addition, sittings for brides (both Gentile and Jewish), family groups, First Holy Communions, and Bar Mitzvahs took place on Saturdays and sittings for Jewish brides also were held on Sundays.

Benjamin Mednick's work exemplifies the family's important role in the economic life of an immigrant who owned his own business. His subjects illustrate the events and people who interacted closely with the photographer and his family.[4]

Left:
Yiddish Theater Group, Molly Picon and Company, Mednick family and friends in Mednick's studio, c. 1935-36
Photograph by Clare (Mednick) Lewin
Courtesy of Clare Lewin and Seymour Mednick

Max Pomerantz was born in Russia in 1862 and emigrated to the United States in 1891. He first settled on Canal Street in New York City and later moved to Philadelphia where he established a studio at 500 South Street. He worked at this address until approximately 1909, when he moved to 700 South Fifth Street. On some of his photographs, which he matted with decorative covers, he advertised as an artistic photographer. Pomerantz used wicker furniture, fur rugs, and other props to create fashionable effects for his sitters. The vast number of his portraits that still exist are indicative of his popularity.

Above:
Cecelia Gerber, 1910
Photograph by Max Pomerantz
Philadelphia Jewish Archives Center at The Balch Institute,
Gift of Tom Sroka

Right:
Unidentified infant,
Cabinent card by Max Pomerantz
Philadelphia Jewish Archives Center at The Balch Institute,
Gift of Hyman Myers

Above:
Elias Goldensky's Philadelphia-Atlantic City Commutation Ticket, 1919
Library Company of Philadelphia

Society of Philadelphia and the Pennsylvania Academy of the Fine Arts in 1898. In 1942 he had a solo exhibition at the former American Museum of Photography (338 South 15th Street, Philadelphia), of which he was a founder. He left to the Museum a large collection of photographs, which eventually were turned over to the International Museum of Photography at George Eastman House. They were included in "An American Century of Photography 1840-1940" sponsored by George Eastman House and held at the Franklin Institute in 1978. In addition, Goldensky was a member of the Photographic Society of Philadelphia, the Commercial Photographers of Philadelphia, and the Miniature Camera Society.[5]

Below:
Naphtali Herz Imber, c. 1909
Photograph by Elias Goldensky
Library Company of Philadelphia

Naphtali Herz Imber, the Austrian Hebrew poet who immigrated to the United States in 1892, wrote "Hatikvah," the Zionist poem which would become the national anthem of the state of Israel.

Another Philadephia portrait photographer, **Elias Goldensky** (1868-1943), became nationally known and was sought out by an elite group of sitters and celebrities. He was born in Russia and came to the United States in 1891 at the age of twenty-three, after declining an offer to become an actor in the Moscow Art Theatre. Five years later he opened a portrait studio at 270 South Third Street, advertising himself as a "modern" photographer. In 1907 he moved from Third Street to 1705 Chestnut Street. Although the range of his work included infant, sibling, and family portraits, his reputation attracted celebrities such as Maxim Gorky, Annette Kellerman, the Morgan dancers, and stars of the grand opera. In 1932 he was called to Hyde Park, New York, to photograph President Roosevelt and his mother. His photographs won awards in Vienna, Paris, London, Dresden, Kiev, and at the St. Louis World's Fair of 1904. Goldensky was a member of the Philadelphia Photographic Salon, and his work appeared in an exhibition sponsored by the Photographic

Above:
Maxim Gorky and Milton Goldensky (Elias' son), 1906
Photograph by Elias Goldensky
Balch Library Collection

Maxim Gorky (1868-1936), the Russian communist author of plays, novels, and memoirs of working class life, visited New York and Philadelphia in 1906.

Right:
Jacob da Silva Solis-Cohen (1838-1927), c. 1884
Photograph by Elias Goldensky
Maxwell Whiteman Collection

Solis-Cohen was a descendant of the first Sephardic Jews (those of Spanish or Portuguese descent) who arrived in New York in 1654. A laryngologist, he published books and articles that made important contributions to the study of the throat and major air passages.

Left:
Domsky-Podolsky family, c. 1890-1910
Cabinent card by Elias Goldensky
Philadelphia Jewish Archives Center at The Balch Institute.
Gift of Mrs. Anna Domsky

Below:
Unidentified Jewish women's group, c. 1910
Photograph by Elias Goldensky
Library Company of Philadelphia

Osias Goldstein was twenty-five in 1906, when he declared his intention to become a citizen of the United States. Born in 1881 in Galatz, Romania, he emigrated aboard the *S.S. Switzerland* of the Red Star Line to Philadelphia. Initially he settled at 331 South Street and moved in 1909 to Max Pomerantz' former studio at 500 South Street.

Right:
Herman and Ida Wechsler, c. 1920
Photograph by Osias Goldstein
Philadelphia Jewish Archives Center at the Balch Institute,
Gift of Anna Harris

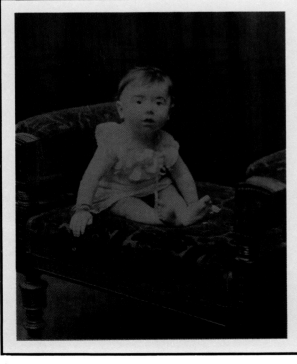

Charles Osias Haimovitz was born in Galatz, Romania, in 1881. He emigrated to the United States from Rotterdam on the vessel *Potsdam* and arrived in New York in April of 1902. Haimovitz declared his intention to become a United States citizen in December 1921 and was naturalized in the Eastern District Court of Pennsylvania in 1926. He had moved to Philadelphia by 1921, residing then at 1729 Memorial Avenue and, five years later, on the "N. W. corner of 16th and Wallace."

Left:
Portrait of unidentified infant, c. 1910-20
Photograph by Charles Osias Haimovitz
Philadelphia Jewish Archives at the Balch Institute,
Gift of Tom Sroka

Daniel Slutsky was born Gedalia Slutsky in 1892 in Poland and came to the United States when he was twelve years old. As a child he worked and went to evening school to learn English. When he had saved enough money to buy his mother and sister steamship tickets, he sent for them to come to America. Having an artistic eye and an intuitive understanding of photography, he quickly adapted to the use of a Brownie camera. He is first listed as a photographer in the Philadelphia city directories for 1914 in partnership with Sam Sax at 2035 7th Street. The two worked together for a year and then Slutsky continued the business on his own. He advertised in *The Forward,* "What's a home without a Slutsky photograph?" His wife recalls that, since many people did not work on Saturdays, they would dress nicely, come to his studio, and wait in line to be photographed. By the time he married T. Sara Cohen in 1919, Slutsky owned two studios, one at 642 Snyder Avenue and the other at 1753 33rd Street. Sara managed the 33rd Street studio.

Above:
Green Family Bar Mitzvah, c. 1910-20,
Photographic postcard by Slutsky's Studio
Philadelphia Jewish Archives Center at The Balch Institute,
Gift of Mrs. Mollie G. Fischer

The Bar Mitzvah is the rite of passage to adulthood of a Jewish boy on his 13th birthday.

Left:
Self-portrait, c. 1930s
Photograph by Daniel Slutsky
Courtesy of T. Sara Slutsky

Above:
Amalgamated Clothing Workers of America Local 148, Dinner, 1940
Photograph by Slutsky's Studios
Urban Archives Center, Temple University

The Amalgamated Clothing Workers of America, a union in the men's clothing industry, provided insurance as well as educational and cultural activities for its members, many of whom were eastern European Jewish immigrants.

Slutsky's studios served the schools in the South Philadelphia area among other customers, and Slutsky pioneered the idea of putting together individual portraits in order to create composite photographs of school classes. Well-liked, willing to travel, and reputed to be an expert photographer, he was even nicknamed "Father Slutsky," and was given a key to the ever-locked St. Charles' seminary, where he took portraits and group sittings for the yearbook.

When the depression slowed business the Slutskys decided that only one studio was needed and sold the 33rd Street studio. Finally in 1948, they sold the studio at 642 Snyder Avenue and the Slutsky name to a fellow photographer.[6]

Jewish photographers living and working in Philadelphia documented many aspects of Jewish communal and cultural life. The events and individuals recorded, both public and private, present Jewish immigrants adapting to American life while holding on to the traditions they cherished. Many of the photographers were immigrants themselves who attempted to bridge old world traditions and new world experiences. Others were descendants of Jewish immigrants. All were intrigued with the ability to preserve images in a tangible and permanent form while maintaining their personal heritage.

Morton Livingston Schamberg (1881-1918) was born in Philadelphia and received a Bachelor's degree in architecture from the University of Pennsylvania. He then attended the Pennsylvania Academy of the Fine Arts at Broad and Cherry Streets in the neighborhood of his home, studying with William Merritt Chase. After graduation he spent time in Europe and returned to Philadelphia, to share a studio at 1626 Chestnut Street with Charles W. Sheeler. Sheeler and Schamberg leased their studio in Philadelphia for just one year and subsequently worked together only during the summer at a studio in Doylestown. Although Schamberg was most noted as a painter, in 1912 or 1913 he and Sheeler both turned to photography in order to support themselves.[7] Schamberg specialized in portrait photography at first, then in 1916 began photographing urban scenes. In 1917 he exhibited his photographs with Sheeler and Paul Strand at the Modern Gallery in New York.[8] The following year he died in the influenza epidemic, two days before his 37th birthday.[9]

Elizabeth Holland *is a graduate of Rutgers, The State University of New Jersey where she studied Art History and Museum Studies. She has served as Research Assistant for the Fairmount Park Art Association, and Curatorial Assistant and Registrar for The Balch Institute.*

Notes

1. See file on Cornelius Levy and Leon Solis-Cohen in the Print Department at the Library Company of Philadelphia.

2. Dumas Malone, *Dictionary of American Biography* (New York: Charles Scribner Sons, 1961), volume VI, p. 203.

3. Interview by author with Reba Stelman, December 12, 1988.

4. Interviews by author with Clare Lewin and Seymour Mednick, 3 December 1988; and Clare Lewin, December 5, 1988

5. See file on Elias Goldensky in the Print Department at the Library Company of Philadelphia.

6. Interview with T. Sara Slutsky, January 12, 1989.

7. Ben Wolf, *Morton Livingston Schamberg* (Philadelphia: University of Pennsylvania Press, 1963), 122.

8. William C. Agee, "Morton Livingston Schamberg: Color and the Evolution of his Painting," in *Morton Livingston Schamberg* (Salander-O'Reilly Gallaries, Inc., 1982), 11, 15.

9. Wolf, 40.

Suggested Reading

Agee, William C. "Morton Livingston Schamberg: Color and the Evolution of his Painting," *Morton Livingston Schamberg.* Salander-O'Reilly Galleries, Inc., 1982.

Hartmann, Sadakichi. "Elias Goldensky," *The Valient Knights of Daguerre: Selected Critical Essays on Photography and Profiles of Photographic Pioneers.* Berkeley: University of California Press, 1978.

Taft, Robert. *Photography and the American Scene: A Social History 1839-1889.* New York: Dover Publications, Inc., 1964.

Welling, William. *Photography in America: The Formative Years: 1839-1900.* New York: Thomas Y. Crowell Co., 1978.

Wolf, Ben. *Morton Livingston Schamberg.* Philadelphia: University of Pennsylvania, 1961.

Note: Dimensions are given in the order of width, height and depth.

A Century of Immigration

1. **Ships' passenger lists, Association of Jewish Immigrants,** 1884-1887
   Bound ledger,
   10 1/2″ x 14 1/2″
   Philadelphia Jewish Archives Center at the Balch Institute. Gift of Hebrew Immigrant Aid Society

2. **Rabbi Wilhelm Sor and his wife Cecilia (Lowenbein) Sor,** Vienna, 1897
   Photographs, each 4″ x 6 1/4″
   Philadelphia Jewish Archives Center at the Balch Institute. Gift of Archibald A. Kalish. Courtesy of Beth Zion/Beth Israel

3. *Tallit* **(prayer shawl)** made in Vienna, worn by Rabbi Wilhelm Sor, c. 1880
   Embroidered silk, 40″ x 82″
   Philadelphia Jewish Archives Center at the Balch Institute. Gift of Archibald A. Kalish. Courtesy of Beth Zion/Beth Israel

4. *Yarmulka* **(prayer cap)** made in Vienna, worn by Rabbi Wilhelm Sor, c. 1880
   Embroidered silk,
   6 1/2″ x 6 1/2″ x 9″
   Philadelphia Jewish Archives Center at the Balch Institute. Gift of Archibald A. Kalish. Courtesy of Beth Zion/Beth Israel

5. *Kiddush* **cup (used to recite the Sabbath prayer over wine)** presented to Rabbi Wilhem Sor in 1892, upon his 40th anniversary as rabbi of a Vienna synagogue
   Engraved silver,
   3″ (diam.) x 6″
   Philadelphia Jewish Archives Center at the Balch Institute. Gift of Archibald A. Kalish. Courtesy of Beth Zion/Beth Israel

6. **Cover for** *matzoh* **(unleavened bread for Passover),** probably made by Massie Silberstein (lender's grandmother) in London, 1888
   Embroidered velvet,
   12 1/2″ x 15″
   Ruth Silberstein Cohen

7. **Esther and Meyer Greenberg (lender's grandmother and grandfather),** c. 1890
   Photographic postcard,
   3 1/2″ x 5 1/2″
   Ruth Silberstein Cohen

8. **Prayer book in German and Hebrew,** 1892
   Owned by Mathilde Steinhardt, who died in the Holocaust
   Printed on paper,
   4 1/2″ x 7 1/4″ x 1/2″
   Balch Museum Collection. Gift of Eileen Voight

9. **M. Rosenbaum, Railroad and Steamship Ticket Agent, business card,** 1897
   Printed on paper, 5″ x 2 3/4″
   Edward W. Rosenbaum

10. **Rosenbaum bank, 603-05 South 3rd Street, (model of *Kronprinzessen Cecile* at left)**, early 20th century
Photograph, 8″ x 5″
Edward W. Rosenbaum

11. **Mortar and pestle brought from Lithuania by Katie Cohen (lender's mother-in-law)**, late 19th century
Copper, 6″ (diam.) x 5 1/2″; 2″ (diam.) x 10″
Pauline Cohen

12. **Sabbath candlesticks brought from Lithuania by Katie Cohen**, late 19th century
Brass, 4 1/4″ (diam.) x 9 1/4″; 3 3/4″ (diam.) x 8 1/2″
Pauline Cohen

13. **Russian samovar**, late 19th century
Brass and wood, 8″ (diam.) x 12″ x 18 3/8″
Mrs. Bert Orodenker

14. **Boonin family portrait**, Slutzk, Russia, taken prior to the emigration of the Boonin children to Philadelphia, 1903
Photograph, 10″ x 8″
The Boonin Family

15. **Letter to Louis Edward Levy, President of the Association for the Protection of Hebrew Immigrants**, from a mother in Russia who seeks the whereabouts of her son in Philadelphia, 1908
Typescript and pencil on paper, 8 1/2″ x 10 3/4″
Maxwell Whiteman Collection

16. **Crocheted needlework coverlet made by a Jewish immigrant from eastern Europe**, 1910
Wool yarn, 56″ x 61″
Balch Museum Collection. Gift of Florence Weiner

17. **Samovar and tea set made by Noah Weinstein (lender's father-in-law)** in Gorodnitza, Ukraine
Gilded porcelain
Samovar: 3″ x 4″ x 6″
Tray: 4″ x 3 1/2″ x 1/4″
Plate: 7″ (diam.) x 1/2″
Teapot: 1 3/4″ x 1 1/4″ x 2″
Sugar bowl: 1 1/2″ x 1″ x 1 3/4″
Teacup: 3/4″ (diam.) x 5/8″
Saucer: 1 1/4″ (diam.) x 1/4″
Creamer: 3/4″ x 1″ x 1 1/4″
Anna Weinstein

18. **World War I journal of Frieda Englander**, Kzernowitz, Austria-Hungary, 1915
Bound volume with postcards and decals pasted on paper, 7 1/2″ x 9 1/2″
Philadelphia Jewish Archives Center at the Balch Institute. Gift of Frieda Englander Flick

19. **Passport of Yetta Reinstein Spritzer, Clara Spritzer Leftwich and Rose Spritzer Schalm**, 22 October, 1920
Printed on paper, 3 1/2″ x 5 1/4″
Philadelphia Jewish Archives Center at the Balch Institute. Leftwich/ Spritzer/Reinstein Family Papers. Gift of Mrs. Clara Leftwich

20. *A South Philadelphia Jew* **by Joseph Sacks**, 1920
Oil on canvas, 19″ x 23″
Maxwell Whiteman Collection

21. **Waiting in the back courtyard at Hebrew Immigrant Aid Society headquarters,** Warsaw, 1921
Photograph by Alter Kacyzne, 9 1/2" x 8"
Philadelphia Jewish Archives Center at the Balch Institute. "Continuity and Change" Collection. Gift of Federation of Jewish Agencies

22. **Laisser-passer from Constantinople for Rosalie and Anna Belsky,** July 6, 1922
Printed form with ink on paper, 8" x 13"
Philadelphia Jewish Archives Center at the Balch Institute. Bell (Belsky) Family Papers. Gift of Anne Prince.

23. **Teapot brought from Russia in 1922 by Doris Anthonofsky (lender's mother)**
Enamel, 3 1/2" (diam.) x 5 1/2"
Pauline Cohen

24. **Charter of Association for the Protection of Jewish Immigrants,** 1927
Ink on paper, 24" x 31 1/2"
Philadelphia Jewish Archives Center at the Balch Institute. Gift of Hebrew Immigrant Aid Society

25. **Bar Mitzvah portrait of Herbert Moser,** Germany, August, 1937
Photograph, 2" x 3"
Herbert and Cyrel Moser

26. **Immigrant identification card ("green card") of Herbert Moser,** 25 May, 1938
Printed on paper with photograph, 5" x 3"
Herbert and Cyrel Moser

27. *Philo Atlas, Handbuch fur die judische auswanderung (Handbook for Jewish Emigrants),* Berlin, 1938
Book, 5 1/2" x 7"
Maxwell Whiteman Collection

Below:
Courtyard of the Hebrew Immigrant Aid Society in Warsaw (Checklist #21)

Right:
Bar mitzvah photo of Herbert Moser (Checklist #25)

Jewish Worship: Orthodoxy and Reform

28. *The Form of Prayers According to the Custom of the Spanish and Portuguese Jews,* edited by Isaac Leeser, 1837
Bound book, 5 3/4" x 9 1/4"
Congregation Mikveh Israel of Philadelphia

29. **Letter to Isaac Leeser,** Kingston, Jamaica, 1858
Ink on paper, 8" x 10"
Maxwell Whiteman Collection

30. **Congregation Mikveh Israel,** 1909
Photograph, 8" x 10"
The Library Company of Philadelphia

31. *Torah* **breastplate (hung in front of the five books of Moses),** inscribed, "Presented by/ Joseph E. Sulzberger/ in memory of his brother/ Jacob Sulzberger/ September 1909"
Silver,
11 1/2" x 21 1/2" x 2 5/8"
Congregation Mikveh Israel of Philadelphia

32. **Ritual ewer,** 1851, inscribed "To/ The Rev'd Isaac Leeser/ from his friends as a testimonial/ of his Zeal and Devotion/ in the cause of Judaism/ in America/ Phila. Adar 5611"
Silver, 8" (diam.) x 17 1/2"
Congregation Mikveh Israel of Philadephia

33. **Charter of the Congregation Beth El Emeth,** 1857
Bound book, 8" x 10 1/4"
Congregation Mikveh Israel of Philadelphia

34. *Commemoration of the 100th Anniversary of The Reverend Dr. Sabato Morais,* 1923
Printed pamphlet, 6 1/2" x 9"
Congregation Mikveh Israel of Philadelphia

35. **The Reverend Leon Elmaleh,** c. 1914
Photograph, 12" x 15 1/2"
Congregation Mikveh Israel of Philadelphia

36. **Burial Records, Levantine Jews Society,** from record book of Mikveh Israel and Beth El Emeth Congregation, 1857 - 1959
Ledger, 8 1/2" x 12 1/2"
Congregation Mikveh Israel of Philadelphia

37. **Admission pass for Miss Mary Burnheimer for consecration of Rodeph Shalom Synagogue building,** 4th Street between Vine and Wood, 4 December, 1843
Cut paper, 5 3/4" x 5"
Museum of Judaica of Congregation Rodeph Shalom

38. **Wimple (swaddling cloth used in the circumcision ceremony)** made in Germany, 1874
Painted cloth, 176" x 8"
Museum of Judaica of Congregation Rodeph Shalom

39. *Attarah* (*tallit* **neckband) worn by Rabbi Mordecai Yahlin,** made in eastern Europe, c. 1890
Embroidered silver threads, 31" x 4 1/4"
Museum of Judaica of Congregation Rodeph Shalom

40. **Container for *etrog* (a citrus fruit used on the Feast of Tabernacles)**
from Palestine, late 19th century
Olive wood,
5 3/4″ x 4″ x 3 1/4″
Museum of Judaica of Congregation Rodeph Shalom

41. **Hanging Sabbath oil lamp made in Germany,** 19th century
Brass,
8 1/4″ (diam.) x 29 1/2″
Museum of Judaica of Congregation Rodeph Shalom

42. **Spice tower used in the *Havdalah* ceremony concluding the Sabbath,** 1926
Silver, 2″ (diam.) x 9 1/2″
Museum of Judaica of Congregation Rodeph Shalom

43. **Sabbath plate,** late 19th century, given as a gift to Rabbi Louis Wolsey in 1940
Porcelain, 13″ x 9″ x 1 3/4″
Museum of Judaica of Congregation Rodeph Shalom

44. **Trowel used by Albert Wolf in laying the cornerstone of the Rodeph Shalom Synagogue,** 18 December, 1927
Engraved silver with ivory handle, 4″ x 12″
Museum of Judaica of Congregation Rodeph Shalom

45. **Keneseth Israel Synagogue,** east side of Broad at Columbia, 1923
Photograph, 4″ x 4″
The Library Company of Philadelphia.

Above:
Keneseth Israel Synagogue (Checklist #45)

46. *Omer* calendar, used to count the 49 days from the second day of Passover to the festival of *Shovuos*, early 20th century
Silver, 5 1/4" x 2" x 5 3/4"
Congregation Keneseth Israel

47. Rev. Joseph Krauskopf, c. 1896
Photograph by Sword, 7 1/2" x 13"
Urban Archives Center, Temple University

48. Draft of sermon by Rev. Joseph Krauskopf, c. 1900
Ink on paper, 8 1/4" x 9 1/2"
Urban Archives Center, Temple University

49. Window with initials "K. I.", Keneseth Israel Synagogue, Broad and Columbia Streets, 1892
Leaded glass, 19 1/2" x 35 3/4" x 2 1/2" (framed)
Congregation Keneseth Israel

50. Door knocker from Keneseth Israel Synagogue,
Broad and Columbia Streets, 1892
Brass, 9" x 16 1/2" (mounted)
Congregation Keneseth Israel

51. *Parokhet* (ark cover) and *kapporet* (valence) from Hevra T'hillim-Bnai Israel Synagogue, Tulip and Auburn Streets, Port Richmond, c. 1905
Velvet, satin, and metallic thread, 96" x 120"
Balch Museum Collection. Gift of Mrs. Bertha Greenberg

52. First *shofar* (ram's horn sounded on the New Year) and bag from the Great Romanian Synagogue, 1886
Shofar: horn, 11" x 5 1/2"
Bag: linen, 27" x 11 1/2"
Society Hill Synagogue

53. Memorial plaque for Sarah Rosner from the Great Romanian Synagogue, 1928
Ink on paper, 12 1/2" x 15 1/2"
Society Hill Synagogue

54. *Tsedakah* (charity) box from the Great Romanian Synagogue
Tin, 3 1/2" 1 1/2" x 4 3/4"
Society Hill Synagogue

55. Door with window from the Great Romanian Synagogue,
418 Spruce Street, 1901-1950
Wood and leaded glass, 40 1/2" x 82 1/2"
Society Hill Synagogue

56. *Tsedakah* (charity) box, made by Herman Blumberg for Congregation B'nai Halberstam, 1917
Copper, 4 1/2" (diam.) x 7 1/2"
Dr. and Mrs. Daniel Blumberg

57. Pair of *teffilin*, containing parchment texts, worn by males at weekday morning prayers
Leather, 2 3/8" x 1 7/8" x 1 1/2" (strap: 132")
Suede bag, 7 1/2" x 8 1/2"
Rita Landau

58. *Tallit* bag given to Louis Cooperson (lender's grandfather) for his Bar Mitzvah, c. 1890
Embroidered velvet, 12 1/2" x 15"
Gladys Gimpel

59. *Tallit Katan* (prayer
    undergarment), c. 1905
    Cotton, 7 1/2″ x 7 1/2″
    Balch Museum Collection.
    Gift of Eleni F. Zatz in
    memory of Clara Gerber
    Lafair
60. **Testimonial given by
    Congregation Dirshu
    Tove to Rev. Joseph Leib
    Mehr,** 1927
    Ink on paper with
    photograph, 26 1/4″ x 32″
    Philadelphia Jewish Archives
    Center at the Balch
    Institute. Archives
    Purchase
61. *Souvenir Dedication
    Exercises of
    Congregation B'nai
    Abraham,* 521-27
    Lombard Street, 3 April,
    1927
    Printed pamphlet,
    6 1/2″ x 9 1/2″
    Philadelphia Jewish Archives
    Center at the Balch
    Institute. B'nai Abraham
    Congregation Records. Gift
    of Mr. and Mrs. Harry
    Block

62. **Record book, Chevra
    Ateres Israel Anshe
    Brahin V'Choimetsch
    (synagogue/beneficial
    society)**
    Bound book with ink, crayon,
    watercolor and gilding on
    paper,
    19 1/2″ x 12 1/2″
    Philadelphia Jewish Archives
    Center at the Balch
    Institute. Gift of Samuel
    Rabinovitz
63. *Kiddush* cup, early 20th
    century
    2″ (diam.) x 2 1/2″
    Balch Museum Collection.
    Gift of Ruth Leppel
64. *Tallit* (prayer shawl) and
    suede bag
    Wool, 17 1/2″ x 51″
    Bag (opened), 9″ x 12 1/2″
    Rita Landau
65. **Green Family Bar Mitzvah,**
    1937
    Photograph by Forward
    Photo Studio,
    5 1/2″ x 8 1/2″
    Philadelphia Jewish Archives
    Center at the Balch
    Institute. Theodore and
    Esther Green Collection.
    Gift of Mollie G. Fischer

Right:
Tsedakah *box from Congregation B'nai
Halberstam* (Checklist #56)

Mutual Assistance and Fellowship

66. **Golden Jubilee plate, Joshua Lodge No. 23, Independent Order of B'nai B'rith,** 30 October, 1905
Ceramic, 9″ (diam.)
Independent Order of B'nai B'rith, Cherry Hill, New Jersey

67. **Ballot box with "black balls," Joshua Lodge no. 23, Independent Order of B'nai B'rith**
Wooden box with marbles, 14 1/2″ x 6″ x 3 1/2″
Independent Order of B'nai B'rith, Cherry Hill, New Jersey

68. **Roll Book of the Max Schermer Lodge No. 3 of the Independent Order Brith Sholom,** 1905-1920
Bound volume, 7″ x 8″
Philadelphia Jewish Archives Center at the Balch Institute. Gift of William Sobel

69. **Beltz-Bessarabia medal awarded to Leopold Schwartz (lender's grandfather) to** commemorate his service as President, 1909
Gold, 1 1/4″ x 1 5/8″
Ernest Schwartz

70. **Beltz-Bessarabia Sick Beneficial Association membership badge**
Metal pin, 2 1/2″ x 1″; Ribbon (with fringe), 2″ x 6″
Ernest Schwartz

Below:
B'nai B'rith ballot box with "black balls"
(Checklist #67)

71. **Beltz-Bessarabia Election Ballot,** 1939
Ink on paper, 8 1/2″ x 12 1/2″
Ernest Schwartz

72. **Prushin-Shershow Lodge No. 132,** 1910
Photograph, 11″ x 14″
Philadelphia Jewish Archives Center at the Balch Institute. Gift of Prushin-Shershow Beneficial Association

73. **Pereyaslaver Progressive Beneficial Association Golden Jubilee book,** 1914
Bound volume, 15″ x 19″
Philadelphia Jewish Archives Center at the Balch Institute. Tobia (Thomas) Reinstein Papers. Gift of Eleanor De Vadetsky

74. **Krivozer Hilfs Farband (beneficial association),** founded 25 December, 1916
Photograph, 11″ x 8″
Philadelphia Jewish Archives Center at the Balch Institute. Gift of Fran Kleiner

75. **Twentieth anniversary souvenir plate, Beltz-Bessarabia Beneficial Association,** 1917
Ceramic, 9″ diameter
Philadelphia Jewish Archives Center at the Balch Institute. Gift of Ernest Schwartz

76. **First Convention of all Berezovker Relief Societies in America and Canada,** 1921
Photograph, 18 1/2″ x 8 1/2″
Philadelphia Jewish Archives Center at the Balch Institute. Gift of Dr. David Rothman

77. **Membership brochure, Samuel I. Vogelson Lodge No. 399, Brith Sholom,** 1933
Printed on paper, 6″ x 7″
Philadelphia Jewish Archives Center at the Balch Institute. Gift of Ben Sturman

78. **Testimonial to President David Landis given by Ahavas Achim Beneficial Association,** 29 January, 1933
Ink on paper with photograph, 28″ x 34″
Boslover Ahavas Achim Beltzer Beneficial Association

79. **Officers and committee of the Kaharliker Beneficial Association,** 1935
Photograph, 14″ x 11″
Philadelphia Jewish Archives Center at the Balch Institute. Kaharliker Beneficial Association Records. Gift of Isadore Trachtenberg

80. **Testimonial to Mr. and Mrs. Charles Cylinder, organizers of the Vitebsker Beneficial Association,** 30 May, 1937
Hand-tinted photograph, 20″ (diam.)
Philadelphia Jewish Archives Center at the Balch Institute. Vitebsker Beneficial Association Records. Gift of David Cylinder.

81. **Show and Dance program, Belz-Bessarabia Beneficial Association,** 25 February, 1940
Printed on paper, 5 3/4″ x 7 3/4″
Philadelphia Jewish Archives Center at the Balch Institute. Gift of Ernest Schwartz

Social Welfare and Philanthropy

82. *Report of the First Annual Dinner of the Hebrew Charitable Fund*,
23 February, 1853
Printed pamphlet, 5 1/2" x 9"
Philadelphia Jewish Archives Center at the Balch Institute. Hebrew Charitable Fund Records. Gift of Edwin Wolf 2nd

83. *First Annual Report of the Jewish Foster Home Society of Philadelphia*, 1856
Printed on paper,
5 3/4" x 8 7/8"
Urban Archives Center, Temple University

84. **Ball dress**, c. 1878
Satin and lace, 18" x 62"
Balch Museum Collection. Gift of Mrs. Harry M. Hyman.

85. **Program for Fête Champêtre, Young Men's Hebrew Association of Philadelphia**, 29 June, 1880
Printed on paper,
5 3/8" x 7 7/8"
Philadelphia Jewish Archives Center at the Balch Institute. Gift of Edwin Wolf 2nd

86. **Dance card, Annual Purim Reception, Young Men's Hebrew Association of Philadelphia**, 19 March, 1884
Printed on paper,
3 1/2" x 5 1/8"
Philadelphia Jewish Archives Center at the Balch Institute. Gift of Edwin Wolf 2nd

87. *Sketch of the Grand March, Hebrew Charity Ball*,
2 February, 1890
Reproduced from *The Sunday Mercury*, 16" x 20"
Philadelphia Jewish Archives Center at the Balch Institute

88. **Charter, The Federation of Jewish Charities of Philadelphia**, 1901
Ink on paper,
32 1/2" x 38 1/2"
Federation of Jewish Agencies of Greater Philadelphia

89. **Program for Concert Evening with Arthur Hartmann, violinist and Alfred Calzin, pianist, Young Men's Hebrew Association**,
28 October, 1907
Printed on paper, 6" x 8"
Philadelphia Jewish Archives Center at the Balch Institute. Leon Obermayer Collection. Gift of Mrs. Leon Obermayer

90. **Gymnasium, Young Women's Union**
Photograph from 1910 Annual Report, 5" x 4"
Philadelphia Jewish Archives Center at the Balch Institute. "Continuity and Change" Collection. Gift of Federation of Jewish Agencies

91. **Shelter, Young Women's Union**
Photograph from 1910 Annual Report, 5" x 4"
Philadelphia Jewish Archives Center at the Balch Institute. "Continuity and Change" Collection. Gift of Federation of Jewish Agencies

92. **Sewing Class, Young Women's Union**
Photograph from 1910 Annual Report, 5" x 4"
Philadelphia Jewish Archives Center at the Balch Institute. "Continuity and Change" Collection. Gift of Federation of Jewish Agencies

93. **"Some of our children in the nursery," Young Women's Union**
Photograph from 1910 Annual Report, 5" x 4"
Philadelphia Jewish Archives Center at the Balch Institute. "Continuity and Change" Collection. Gift of Federation of Jewish Agencies

94. **Doily made in sewing class, Young Women's Union**,
early 20th century
Embroidered cotton,
21" (diam.)
Philadelphia Jewish Archives Center at the Balch Institute. Gift of Mrs. Esther Shapiro

95. **Child posing in Russian costume, Neighborhood Day Nursery**, c. 1910
Photographic postcard,
3 1/2" x 5 1/2"
Philadelphia Jewish Archives Center at the Balch Institute. Gift of Neighborhood Centre

96. **South Philadelphia street scene** (possibly a day nursery class), c. 1910
Photograph, 10" x 8"
Philadelphia Jewish Archives Center at the Balch Institute. "Continuity and Change" Collection. Gift of Federation of Jewish Agencies

97. **Samuel S. Fels**
    Photograph, 5″ x 7″
    Samuel S. Fels Fund

98. **Advertising flyer for Young Men's and Women's Hebrew Association Building Campaign,**
    30 October - 8 November, 1921
    Printed on paper, 17 1/2″ x 9 1/4″
    Philadelphia Jewish Archives Center at the Balch Institute. Leon Obermayer Collection. Gift of Mrs. Leon Obermayer

99. **"Outside Jewish Neighborhood House on trip to Overbrook School for the Blind",** Saturday, 5 June, 1926
    Photograph, 10″ x 8″
    Philadelphia Jewish Archives Center at the Balch Institute. Gift of Neighborhood Centre

100. **Foster Home, Juvenile Aid Society,** c. 1935
    Photograph, 10″ x 7 1/2″
    Philadelphia Jewish Archives Center at the Balch Institute. Gift of Association for Jewish Children

101. **American League Championship, South Philadelphia Hebrew Athletic Society,** 1936-37
    Ink on drawing board by F. D. Warren, 18″ x 12 3/4″
    Philadelphia Jewish Archives Center at the Balch Institute. Eddie Gottlieb Collection. Gift of Dave Zinkoff

102. **Basketball team, Foster Home for Hebrew Orphans,** 1937-38
    Photograph, 10″ x 8″
    Philadelphia Jewish Archives Center at the Balch Institute. Gift of Association for Jewish Children

Below:
American League Championship, SPHAS
(Checklist #101)

Entering the Mainstream

103. *The Persecution of the Jews in the East, containing the Proceedings of a meeting held at the Synagogue Mikveh Israel,* Philadelphia, 27 August, 1840
Pamphlet, 6 1/4" x 10"
Library Company of Philadelphia

104. **"The Chosen People," political cartoon by J. Keppler,** 1880
From *Puck,* 19 7/8" x 13 7/8"
Balch Library Collection. Library Purchase

105. **"Am I an Anti-Semite?" 9 Addresses by Rev. Charles E. Coughlin,** 6 November, 1938 - 1 January, 1939
Clothbound book, published by the Condon Printing Co., Detroit, 5" x 7"
Balch Library Collection. Library Purchase

106. **Letter to radio host Patrick Stanton, protesting the censorship of Rev. Coughlin's broadcasts by WDAS,** 4 December, 1938
Ink on paper, 6 1/2" x 10"
Balch Library Collection. Patrick J. Stanton Papers

107. **Civil War commission of Rev. Jacob Frankel,** signed by Abraham Lincoln, April 22, 1863
Printed certificate, 13 1/2" x 18"
Museum of Judaica of Congregation Rodelph Shalom

108. **"Food Will Win the War"** U. S. Government WWI Conservation poster (in Yiddish)
Lithograph, 21 1/2" x 31 3/4"
Balch Museum Collection. Museum Purchase

109. **The Ladies of the Order of the Eastern Star,** Lansford, PA, c. WWI
Photograph, 10" x 8"
Philadelphia Jewish Archives Center at the Balch Institute. Gift of Jennie and Judy Rotman

110. **Charter of Philadelphia Post No. 13, Jewish War Veterans,** 2 June, 1919
Printed certificate, 20 3/4" x 17 7/8"
Balch Museum Collection. Museum Purchase

Hospitals and Health Care

111. *Notice of the Committee established for the purpose of founding a Jewish Hospital,* 18 August, 1864
Printed broadside, 10" x 8"
Library Company of Philadelphia

112. **Tea and coffee service (4 pieces from a 6 piece set),** made by Robert and William Wilson
Inscribed: "Presented to Rev. J. Frankel by his friends at the Jewish Hospital Fair under the auspices of the YMDA [Young Men's Dramatic Association], Philadelphia, January 20, 1866"
Engraved silver plate
Coffee pot: 11 1/4" x 11 3/4"
Covered sugar bowl: 8 3/4" x 9 1/2"
Creamer: 5 1/4" x 7 3/4"
Footed spill bowl: 5 1/4" x 5 1/2"
Museum of Judaica of Congregation Rodeph Shalom

113. *Laying of the cornerstone of the Jewish Hospital,* 9 October, 1872
Printed pamphlet, 5 1/2" x 8 1/2"
Urban Archives Center, Temple University

114. **"The Golden Book of Life," receipt for donation made by Lucien Moss to the Jewish Hospital,** 15 September, 1873
Printed on paper, 8 5/8" x 5"
Philadelphia Jewish Archives Center at the Balch Institute. Albert Einstein Medical Center Collection. Gift of Edwin Wolf 2nd

115. ***Tenth Annual Report, Jewish Hospital Association,*** 1875
Printed pamphlet, 5 7/8″ x 9″
Urban Archives Center, Temple University

116. ***Programme for the Dedication of the Lucien Moss Home for Incurables,*** 10 June 1900
Printed on paper, 6″ x 9″
Philadelphia Jewish Archives Center at the Balch Institute. Albert Einstein Medical Center Collection. Gift of Edwin Wolf 2nd

117. **Sun parlor at the Home for Aged and Infirm Israelites, the Jewish Hospital,** c. 1900
Photograph, 10″ x 8″
Balch Library Collection. Albert Einstein Medical Center Collection

118. ***Souvenir Journal, First Annual Ball,*** **Mount Sinai Hospital,** at Musical Fund Hall, 1901
Printed pamphlet, 4 1/8″ x 9 1/4″
Philadelphia Jewish Archives Center at the Balch Institute. Gift of Mrs. Eleanor Gilbert

Below:
Sun parlor, Home for Aged and Infirm Israelites
(Checklist #117)

119. **Children's ward at Mt. Sinai Hospital,** 1928
Photograph, 10″ x 8″
Balch Library Collection.
Albert Einstein Medical
Center Collection

120. **Jewish Maternity Home ward,** 534 Spruce Street, c. 1910
Photograph, 9 3/4″ x 7 1/2″
Philadelphia Jewish Archives
Center at the Balch
Institute. Julius H. and
Carrie Amram Greenstone
Papers. Gift of Mrs. Gella
Kraus

121. **Carrie Amram Greenstone with daughter Leah**
Photograph by Franz
Meynen, 4 1/4″ x 6″
Philadelphia Jewish Archives
Center at the Balch
Institute. Julius H. and
Carrie Amram Greenstone
Papers. Gift of Mrs. Gella
Kraus

122. **Bertha Amram**
Photograph, 2 3/4″ x 5 1/4″
Philadelphia Jewish Archives
Center at the Balch
Institute. Julius H. and
Carrie Amram Greenstone
Papers. Gift of Mrs. Gella
Kraus

123. **Northern Liberties Hospital representatives with Eleanor Roosevelt,** 1938
Photograph by Milton Jay
Stander, 9 3/4″ x 8″
Philadelphia Jewish Archives
Center at the Balch
Institute. Louis and Bertha
Gershenfeld Papers

124. **Cataract knife invented and used by Isaac Hays**
Steel and plastic,
4 3/8″ x 1/8″
Mutter Museum of the
College of Physicians

125. **Electric cautery handle owned by Dr. Jacob da Silva Solis-Cohen**
Brass and wood, 6 1/4″ x 5/8″
Mutter Museum of the
College of Physicians

126. **Apothecary scales owned by Dr. Isaac Hays**
Steel and brass
Beam: 4 5/8″ long;
Pans: 1 5/8″ diam.; [hanging
configuration, 5 1/2″ x 1
5/8″ x 7″]
Mutter Museum of the
College of Physicicans

127. **Camera for laryngeal photos invented by Dr. Jacob da Silva Solis-Cohen**
Wood, brass, steel and
mirrored glass
Body: 10 1/2″ x 1 1/2″ x 7/8″
Lens: 7/8″ (diam.) x 2 1/8″
Mutter Museum of the
College of Physicians

128. **Jacob da Silva Solis-Cohen, M.D., L.L.D.,** 1924
Photograph by Elias
Goldensky (signed),
11″ x 13 1/4″
Maxwell Whiteman
Collection

129. **Mr. and Mrs. Leybele Satanoffsky and family**
c. 1885
Cabinet card by Max
Pomerantz, 4 1/4″ x 6 1/2″
Philadelphia Jewish Archives
Center at the Balch
Institute. Leybele
Satanoffsky Family
Records. Gift of Mrs. Edith
Satanoff

Family Traditions

130. *Menorah* (Hanukkah lamp)
made in Lodz, Poland by
lender's grandfather in
1881
Silver, 8 7/8" x 2 1/4" x 6 3/4"
National Museum of
American Jewish History.
Gift of Rebecca Jarvis

131. **Sabbath bonnet worn in
Berlin, Germany by
Rosalie Hirschberg
Lövinson (lender's
grandmother),** c. 1850
Cotton, 10" x 8"
Museum of Judaica of
Congregation Rodeph
Shalom

132. **Ewer engraved, "J. and C.
Joseph to R. and A.
Joseph/January 2nd,
1867"**
Silver, 6 1/2" x 5" x 12 3/4"
Mr. and Mrs. Frank P.
Louchheim

133. **Russian salt dish,** 1873
Silver, 2 1/8" (diam.) x 1 1/2"
Graboyes/Segal Family

134. **Russian *kiddush* cup,** 1873
Silver, 2 1/4" (diam.) x 2 3/8"
Graboyes/Segal Family

135. **Autograph book of Caroline
Amram,** 1879
Ink on paper, 4" x 4 1/4"
Philadelphia Jewish Archives
Center at the Balch
Institute. Julius H. and
Carrie Amram Greenstone
Papers. Gift of Mrs. Gella
Kraus

136. **Russian cloth, used to
drape family pictures as
a memorial tribute,**
c. 1889
Embroidered linen,
80" x 15 1/4"
Balch Museum Collection.
Given in memory of Bessie
Maranees Subkis by her
daughter and
granddaughter Jennie and
Judy Rotman

137. **Russian cloth, used to
drape family pictures,**
c. 1890
Embroidered linen,
80" x 15 1/4"
Balch Museum Collection.
Given in memory of Bessie
Maranees Subkis by her
daughter and
granddaughter Jennie and
Judy Rotman.

138. **The Melinson Family at
home in Ledger Place**
(adjacent to American
Street), late 1890s
Cabinet card by E. Hafen,
4 1/4" x 6 1/2"
Philadelphia Jewish Archives
Center at the Balch
Institute. Gift of Jennie and
Judy Rotman

139. **Russian pot,** c. 1890
Copper, 12" (diam.) x 7 1/2"
Graboyes/Segal Family

140. **Russian bowl,** c. 1890
Brass, 15" (diam.) x 4"
Graboyes/Segal Family

141. **Mordecai Bateman
(lender's grandfather),**
1890s
Lithograph with pencil
drawing, 20 1/4" x 24 1/4"
Maxwell Whiteman
Collection

Right:
Tovia Whiteman with New Year's greeting card
(Checklist #162)

Above:
Edgar S. Bamburger, Mildred Daisy Fox and Walter Fox (Checklist #147)

142. ***Ketubah* (marriage contract) of Lev Hirshler and Carrie Frechie,** 1894
Ink on parchment,
6 3/8″ x 10 3/4″
National Museum of
American Jewish History.
Gift of Dr. Sylvester Miller

143. **Circumcision dress,** 1898
Cotton, 18″ x 21″
Dr. and Mrs. Daniel
Blumberg

144. **Kater Street,** June 1910
Photograph, 3 1/8″ x 4 1/8″
Urban Archives Center,
Temple University

145. **"The Ghosts of My Friends," autograph book,** 1910
Bound book with autographs
in ink, 4″ x 6 3/4″
Rosenbach Museum and
Library

146. **Daisy Fox Bamberger,** 1910
Photograph, 7″ x 9″
Lee Leopold

147. **Edgar S. Bamberger, Mildred Daisy Fox and Walter Fox,** 1910
Photographic postcard,
3 1/2″ x 5 1/2″
Lee Leopold

148. **Morris and Jennie Wollod,** c. 1910
Photograph, 8″ x 10″
Alex Wollod

149. **Gertrude Maranees Sakin,** 1912
Photograph by Charles D.
Marrison, 13 7/8″ x 18 3/4″
Balch Museum Collection.
Gift of Jennie and Judy
Rotman

150. **Post card with *Rosh Hashanah* (New Year's) greetings,** c. 1910
Color photograph, 8″ x 9 7/8″
National Museum of
American Jewish History.
Gift of Marilyn Glass

151. **Postcard with New Year's greetings,** 1915
Color photograph.
Inscription on reverse,
8″ x 9 7/8″
National Museum of
American Jewish History.
Museum Purchase

152. **Joseph Stein and Max Harrison in Atlantic City,** 1912
Photographic postcard by
Holt's Studio,
3 1/2″ x 5 1/2″
Sylvia Stein

153. **Gertrude M. and Mortin Rotman,** c. 1912
Photographic postcard,
3 1/2″ x 5 1/2″
Philadelphia Jewish Archives
Center at the Balch
Institute. Gift of Jennie and
Judy Rotman

154. **Lipe Segal,** 1900
Photograph, 5″ x 7″
Graboyes/Segal Family

155. **Laike Segal,** 1900
Photograph, 5″ x 7″
Graboyes/Segal Family

156. **Wedding of Esther and Morris Rosenberg (lender's parents),** 1917
Photographic postcard,
4″ x 6″
Ruth Leppel

157. **Sugar bowl, wedding gift to Minnie and David Prager,** 1917
Silver plate,
8″ x 5 1/2″ x 7 3/4″
Stella P. Cotzer

158. **Circumcision knife and box,** 1920
Steel and ivory. Box:
6 1/2″ x 1″ x 1/2″
Museum of Judaica of
Congregation Rodeph
Shalom

Above:
Joseph Stein and Max Harrison (Checklist #152)

159. **Durfor Street, Mifflin Square in background,** early 20th century
Photograph, 9 3/4″ x 7 1/2″
Urban Archives Center, Temple University

160. **Album with Hilsum family photographs taken at home at 2425 N. Carlisle Street,** c. 1920
Photographs glued on craft paper (bound), 7″ x 5 1/4″ x 3/4″
Gail F. Stern

161. **Morris and Esther Rosenberg and family,** 1924
Photograph, 20″ x 15 3/4″
Ruth Leppel

162. **Tovia Whiteman (lender's father) with New Year's greeting card,** 1924
Lithograph and card, 9 1/2″ x 15 1/2″ (framed together)
Maxwell Whiteman Collection

163. **Russian Jewish doll,** c. 1925
Cotton cloth, 6 1/2″ x 12″
Balch Museum Collection. Gift of Betty Ewen

164. **Russian Jewish doll,** c. 1925
Cotton cloth, 6 1/2″ x 12″
Balch Museum Collection. Gift of Betty Ewen

165. **Prayerbook presented to Anna Graboyes Segal,** on the occasion of the *brith milah* (circumcision ceremony) of her son, Albert Segal, 1927
3 1/2″ x 4 3/4″
Graboyes/Segal Family

166. **Invitation to *brith milah* of Albert Segal,** 1927
Postcard, 5 1/2″ x 3 1/4″
Graboyes/Segal Family

Below:
Laike and Lipe Segal (Checklist #155 and #154)

Above:
Page from Hilsum family photo album
(Checklist #160)

Below:
Morris and Esther Rosenberg and family
(Checklist #161)

Through the Eyes of Jewish Photographers

167. **"Views in and around Richmond", 1865:** *Libby Prison, View of Burnt District, Ruins of the Arsenal*
Cartes de visite by Levy and Solis-Cohen, each 3 3/4″ x 2 1/4″
Library Company of Philadelphia

168. **Levy and Solis-Cohen self-portrait,** c. 1865
Photograph 10″ x 8″
Library Company of Philadelphia

169. *The Mercury: An Illustrated Newspaper,* **showing Levytype photoengravings,**
1 December, 1889,
13″ x 18 1/4″
Maxwell Whiteman Collection

170. **Memorial Program for Louis Edward Levy, under the auspices of the Jewish Community of Philadelphia,**
23 March, 1919,
Printed on paper,
5 3/8″ x 7 3/4″
Maxwell Whiteman Collection

171. **Domsky-Podolsky family,** c. 1890-1910
Cabinet card by Elias Goldensky,
4 3/16″ x 6 9/16″
Philadelphia Jewish Archives Center at the Balch Institute. Gift of Mrs. Anna Domsky

172. **Naphtali Herz Imber,** c. 1898
Photograph by Elias Goldensky, 7″ x 9″
Library Company of Philadelphia

173. **Leon Creamer,** c. 1900
Glass color plate photograph attributed to Elias Goldensky
7 1/8″ x 7 1/4″ x 9 1/4″
Philadelphia Jewish Archives Center at the Balch Institute. Gift of Mrs. Bea Creamer

174. **Maxim Gorky and Milton Goldensky (the photographers' son),** 1906
Photograph by Elias Goldensky, 3 3/4″ x 5 3/4″
Balch Institute Library Collection. Joseph Paull Photographs

175. **Unidentified Jewish women's group,** c. 1910
Photograph by Elias Goldensky, 9 3/8″ x 7 5/8″
Library Company of Philadelphia

Below:
Joseph Rotman and his brother (Checklist #176)

102

176. **Joseph Rotman and his brother**
Cabinet card by Elias Goldensky, 5 1/8″ x 7 1/8″
Philadelphia Jewish Archives Center at the Balch Institute. Gift of Jennie and Judy Rotman

177. **Commutation ticket owned by Elias Goldensky,** 1919
Printed on card with photograph, 4 1/8″ x 2 5/8″
Library Company of Philadelphia

178. **T. Sara Slutsky,** 1917
Photograph with color pencil embellishment by Daniel Slutsky
5 1/8″ x 11″
T. Sara Slutsky

179. **Green Family Bar Mitzvah,** c. 1910-20
Photographic postcard by Slutsky's Studio,
3 3/8″ x 5 3/8″
Philadelphia Jewish Archives Center at the Balch Institute. Theodore and Esther Green Collection. Gift of Mollie G. Fischer

180. **Self portrait by Daniel Slutsky,** c. 1930's
Photograph, 3 1/4″ x 4 5/8″
T. Sara Slutsky

181. **Nettis Family,** c. 1935-38
Photograph attributed to Slutsky Studios, 8″ x 10″
Morris A. Nettis

182. **Cecilia Gerber,** 1910
Photograph by Max Pomerantz, 5 7/8″ x 8 7/8″
Philadelphia Jewish Archives Center at the Balch Institute. Gift of Tom Sroka

183. **New Year's card with photo of unidentified infant,** c. 1910-20
Cabinet card by Max Pomerantz, 4 1/2 ″ x 6 1/2″
Philadelphia Jewish Archives Center at the Balch Institute. Gift of Hyman Myers

184. **Unidentified child,** c. 1910-20
Photograph by Charles Osias Haimovitz, 6 1/8″ x 10 1/8″
Philadelphia Jewish Archives Center at the Balch Institute. Gift of Tom Sroka

185. **Self-portrait by Morton Livingston Schamberg in Chestnut Street studio,** c. 1913
Photograph, 11″ x 12 1/4″
Ruth and Ben Wolf

186. **Jennye Whitehill Greenberg,** c. 1913
Photograph by Morton Livingston Schamberg, 8″ x 10″
Ruth and Ben Wolf

187. **Business card of B. Mednick, artist,** c. 1914
Printed on paper, 3 3/4″ x 2 3/16″
Clare Lewin and Seymour Mednick

188. **Hymie Prizant and his niece Mildred,** 1920
Photograph by Benjamin Mednick, 5 7/8″ x 4″
Clare Lewin and Seymour Mednick

189. **Clare's Halloween Party,** 1926
Photograph by Benjamin Mednick, 7″ x 5″
Clare Lewin and Seymour Mednick

190. **Class of the I. L. Peretz School under the sponsorship of the Workmen's Circle,** 1930-31
Photograph by Benjamin Mednick, 10 3/4″ x 9 1/2″
Clare Lewin and Seymour Mednick

191. **Seymour's birthday party,** 1931
Photograph by Benjamin Mednick, 10″ x 8″
Clare Lewin and Seymour Mednick

192. **Mednick family portrait,** 1933
Photograph by Benjamin Mednick, 7 7/8″ x 9 7/8″
Clare Lewin and Seymour Mednick

193. **Molly Picon and theatre group, Mednick family and friends,** 1935-36
Photograph by Clare Mednick, 10″ x 8″
Clare Lewin and Seymour Mednick

194. **Herman and Ida Wechsler,** c. 1920
Photograph by Osias Goldstein, 7″ x 9 7/8″
Philadelphia Jewish Archives Center at the Balch Institute. Gift of Anna Harris

195. **Stelman children in family car,** 1938
Photograph by Jacob Stelman, 5″ x 4″
Harriet Joyce Epstein

196. **President Roosevelt in Philadelphia,** 1940
Photograph by Jacob Stelman, 8 1/8″ x 10″
Harriet Joyce Epstein

197. **"Stelman Studios Commercial Photography"**
Advertisement by Jacob Stelman, 11″ x 14″
Harriet Joyce Stelman

198. **Self-portrait with camera by Jacob Stelman,** 1956
Photograph, 7″ x 7 3/4″
Harriet Joyce Epstein

Culture and the Arts

199. **The Occident and American Jewish Advocate,** published by Isaac Leeser, May 1857
Printed pamphlet, 5 1/2" x 9"
Congregation Mikveh Israel of Philadelphia

200. **Jewish Publication Society 10th Anniversary souvenir menu,** May 22, 1898
Leather, 2 3/4" x 4 1/4"
Philadelphia Jewish Archives Center at the Balch Institute. Gift of Edwin Wolf 2nd

201. **The Philadelphia Jewish Morning News,** 3 April, 1907
Newspaper, 15 1/2" x 21"
Philadelphia Jewish Archives Center at the Balch Institute. Gift of Mona Weinberg

202. **Morris Rosenbaum's Library at 1821 Diamond Street**
Photograph, 10" x 8"
Edward W. Rosenbaum

203. **The Schiff Classics Committee, Jewish Publication Society,** c. 1916
Photograph, 13" x 10 1/4"
Philadelphia Jewish Archives Center at the Balch Institute. Gift of Jewish Publication Society

Below:
Library of Morris Rosenbaum, 1821 Diamond Street (Checklist #202)

104

204. **Programme for "Hebrew Literature Society - Commercial School Commencement Exercises,"** 24 February, 1920
Printed on paper,
3 3/4" x 6 1/4"
Philadelphia Jewish Archives Center at the Balch Institute. Gift of Ben Beitchman

205. *Crossroads (Shaidweg),* 1935
By Barrish Eppelbaum
Bound book, 6 1/4" x 9 1/4"
Private Collection

206. **"Kultur Bookstore" business card,** late 1930s
Printed on paper,
3 3/8" x 1 7/8"
Private Collection

207. *The Juvenile Stage: A History of the Yiddish Hebrew Dramatic Societies, 1890-1940,* by David B. Tierkel
Bound book, 6 1/2" x 9 1/4"
Private collection

208. **"Kosher Kitty Kelly" advertisement for a dramatic performance, Franklin Theater**
Printed on paper,
5 1/2" x 9 1/4"
Philadelphia Jewish Archives Center at the Balch Institute. Abraham Hofferman Papers. Gift of Mrs. Abraham Hofferman

209. **Miniature Playhouse Players (group portrait),** February 1917
Photograph by Slutsky's Studio, 10" x 7 1/2"
Philadelphia Jewish Archives Center at the Balch Institute. Oscar I. and Edith Levin Stern Collection

Above:
Crossroads *by Barrish Eppelbaum* (Checklist #205)

Above:
Arch Street Theatre poster (Checklist #211)

210. **Honorary Evening for Ludwig Satz,** 22 March, 1917
Arch Street Theater poster, 27″ x 42″
American Jewish Historical Society

211. **"Apartment Three,"** 23 March, 1917
Arch Street Theater poster, 28″ x 42″
American Jewish Historical Society

212. **"Die Liebe,"** 1923
Arch Street Theater sheet music, 9 1/4″ x 12 1/4″
Mrs. Norma Tarnoff

213. **"A Nest of Love"**
Arch Street Theater sheet music, 9 1/4″ x 12 1/4″
Mrs. Norma Tarnoff

214. **Playbill for "The Golem" presented by the Moscow Theater,** Metropolitan Opera House, 24 February 1927
Printed on paper, 6 1/4″ x 9 3/8″
Philadelphia Jewish Archives Center at the Balch Institute. Gift of Edith Deitch

215. **Broadside for a Grand One-Act Play Contest and Forum,** Jewish Education Center No. 1, 508 Moore Street, 30 March, 1930
Photograph, 6 3/4″ x 10 3/4″
Balch Library Collection. Joseph Paull Papers

216. **Performance at Girls' High School by the evening English class for immigrants,** c. 1930
Photograph, 9 1/2″ x 7 1/2″
Terry B. Horowitz

217. ***Sheindele the Chazente,***
WDAS Radio
Broadside, 9" x 12"
Philadelphia Jewish Archives
Center at the Balch
Institute. Jean Gornish
Collection. Gift of Sylvia
Silver

218. Gown, stole and cap worn
by Sheindele the
Chazente during radio
performances, c. 1930
Silk blend
Gown: 38" x 53 1/2"
Stole: 6 1/2" x 10 1/4"
Cap: 7" x 7" x 7 1/2"
Balch Museum Collection.
Gift of Sylvia Silver

219. Broadside for Purim
Concert, 1930
Printed on paper, 5 3/4" x 11"
National Museum of
American Jewish History.
Gift of Sondra Katz

220. Picnic of the Jewish Foster
Home and Orphan
Asylum, at the site of the
Religious Liberty Statue,
Fairmount Park,
24 August, 1897
Photograph by R. Newell and
Son, 9 1/2" x 7 1/2"
Philadelphia Jewish Archives
Center at the Balch
Institute. Gift of
Association for Jewish
Children

Below:
Detail, broadside for a Grand One-Act Play
Contest, Jewish Education Center No. 1
(Checklist #215)

PURIM CONCERT

Given by the

JEWISH COMER STUDIO OF PHILA.

on Sunday Evening, March 16th, 1930, at 8 o'clock

at Pottstown Jewish Community Center

I.

PLAYLET IN ONE ACT.

"TRAGEDY OF SPASS"

⁜

CAST OF CHARACTERS

MRS. ORANSTEIN	Mrs. Eva Letofsky
LENA, HER DAUGHTER	Ida Lewis
HER FIANCE	Ruben Muller
THE BOARDER	Jack London
THE MARRIAGE-MAKER	Jack Rosen

II.

PIANO SELECTIONS	Jack Jaffe
SONGS	Ida Shnitzer
JEWISH FOLK SONGS	Ruben Muller
A RECITATION	Ida Lewis
FOLK SONGS	Morris Miller

III.

TRIO SKETCH, "THE DUMMY"

PLAYED BY:

THE JUDGE	Jack Rosen
THE INTERPRETER	Ruben Muller
THE DEAF AND DUMB	Al Shnitzer

IV.

TRIO SONG "A-KIND-UN-A-HEIM" { Jack Rosen / Ruben Muller / Ida Schnitzer

V.

THE CITIZEN PAPERS Given By { Jack Rosen / Al Shnitzer

DIRECTED BY MR. LEON NOVAK

STAGE DIRECTOR and PROMPTER, MR. BARRISH.

MUSIC PLAYED COMPOSED BY MR. JACK JAFFE.

EDWARD LETOFSKY
Business Manager

Jewish Comer Studio
of Philadelphia

221. ***Appeal of the Constitution Grand Lodge to the membership of B'nai B'rith to support a fundraising drive for "Religious Liberty" by Moses Ezekiel*** (in English and German), January, 1875
Printed on paper, 8 1/2″ x 11″
B'nai B'rith International

222. ***Programme of ceremonies at the unveiling of "Religious Liberty" by Moses Ezekiel,*** 30 November, 1876
Printed on paper, 6″ x 9″
B'nai B'rith International

223. **Samuel Fleisher,** c. 1920
Engraving by Harry S. Moskovitz, 7″ x 9″
Mr. and Mrs. Frank P. Louchheim

224. **Helen Fleisher,** c. 1920s
Photograph by Phillips, 11 3/4″ x 16 1/2″
Mr. and Mrs. Frank P. Louchheim

225. ***The Immigrants* by Raphael Soyer**
Lithograph, 24 1/2″ x 25 1/2″
Balch Museum Collection. Museum Purchase

226. **Poster advertising Ellen Phillips Samuel Memorial Exhibition,** 1940
Silkscreen on paper, 12″ x 17″
Fairmount Park Art Association

227. **Cameramen of Lubin's Co. Studios,** 20th and Indiana Aves., c. 1910
Photograph, 3 5/8″ x 9 7/8″
Free Library of Philadelphia. Lubin Archives

Left:
Purim concert broadside (Checklist #219)

The Tradition of Learning

228. *Report of the Hebrew Education Society of Philadelphia*, 1885
Printed on paper, 5 3/4″ x 9″
Library Company of Philadephia

229. *Fifty Years' Work of the Hebrew Education Society of Philadelphia 1848-1898*, published by the Society, 1899
Bound book, 6 1/4″ x 9 1/2″
Gratz College Library

230. Hyman Gratz (1776 - 1857)
Levytype photoengraving, 5 7/8″ x 9 3/8″
Maxwell Whiteman Collection

231. Gratz College examination in Hebrew, June 1901
Ink on paper, 8″ x 10″
Philadelphia Jewish Archives Center at the Balch Institute. Julius H. and Carrie Amram Greenstone Papers. Gift of Mrs. Gella Kraus

232. Beth Israel Confirmation Class, 1910
Photograph by Elias Goldensky, 14″ × 11½″
Philadelphia Jewish Archives Center at the Balch Institute, Gift of Lillian Sacks Haber

233. Moses A. Dropsie (1821 - 1905)
Photograph, 8″ x 10″
Maxwell Whiteman Collection

234. Ellen Phillips medal awarded to Nathan Luzner, Hebrew Sunday School, 5 June, 1904
Silver, 1″ (diam.)
Philadelphia Jewish Archives Center at the Balch Institute. Hebrew Sunday School Society, Ellen Phillips School Collecton. Gift of Mrs. Albert Toll

235. Ellen Phillips medal awarded to Elsie Luzner, Hebrew Sunday School,
June 3, 1906
Silver, 1 1/4″ diam.
Philadelphia Jewish Archives Center at the Balch Institute. Gift of Mrs. Albert Toll

236. Medal commemorating 75th Anniversary of the Hebrew Sunday School Society, Philadelphia, 2 March, 1913
Button, 7/8″ (diam.)
Ribbon, 1″ x 2″
Philadelphia Jewish Archives Center at the Balch Institute. Gift of Mrs. Hannah Green Bergman

Right:
Portrait of Moses Dropsie (Checklist #233)

Above:
Medal commemorating 75th anniversary of the Hebrew Sunday School Society (Checklist #236)

237. **Gordon Behal Hirsh Medal awarded to Hannah Green by the Hebrew Sunday School Society,** c. 1915
Gold metal, 1 3/8″ x 1/2″
Philadelphia Jewish Archives Center at the Balch Institute. Gift of Mrs. Hannah Green Bergman

238. **Medal awarded to Hannah Green, Germantown Hebrew Sunday School,** 6 June, 1915
Gold metal, 1″ x 1 1/4″
Philadelphia Jewish Archives at the Balch Institute. Gift of Mrs. Hannah Green Bergman

239. **Classroom of Keneseth Israel Religious School,** c. 1904-05
Photograph, 19 3/4″ x 16″
Balch Museum Collection

240. **Brick certificate, Central Hebrew Free School,** 1911
Printed on paper, 11″ x 8 1/2″
Congregation Mikveh Israel of Philadelphia

241. **Hebrew Sunday School Society Pupil's Roll Book,** 1816 Chestnut Street, 1915
Bound book, 6 1/2″ x 6 3/4″
Philadelphia Jewish Archives Center at the Balch Institute. Gift of Mrs. Leon Obermayer

242. ***A History of the United States*, by Allen C. Thomas, A. M.,** 1916, owned by Maurice Merion (lender's grandfather)
Book in English and Yiddish, 6″ x 8 1/4″
Lent by Bennett and Mildred Merion

243. **Hebrew Literature Society Sunday School Graduating Class,** 1920
Photograph, 10″ x 8″
Miriam B. Grobman and Harry D. Boonin

244. **Scrapbook, Isabella Rosenbach Vacation School** (under the auspices of the Hebrew Sunday School Society), 8 July - 15 August, 1935
Ink and crayon on drawing paper, 11″ x 13″
Rosenbach Museum and Library

245. **Neighborhood House Progress School (boys),** 1935
Photograph, 3 1/2″ x 2 1/2″
Philadelphia Jewish Archives Center at the Balch Institute. Gift of Neighborhood Centre

246. **Neighborhood House Progress School (girls),** 1935
Photograph, 3 1/2″ x 2 1/2″
Philadelphia Jewish Archives Center at the Balch Institute. Gift of Neighborhood Centre

247. ***Folkshul* certificate of Miriam Zevin, Mendele Mocher Sforim Folkshul,** 24 June 1938
Ink on paper, 9 1/4″ x 12 3/4″
Philadelphia Jewish Archives Center at the Balch Institute. Gift of Miriam Zevin Brillman

248. **School absentee notice in English and Yiddish,** early 20th century
Printed on card stock. 5 1/2″ x 3 1/2″
Philadelphia Jewish Archives Center at The Balch Institute. Gift of Rakhmiel Peltz

Right:
*Hebrew Literature Society Sunday School
graduating class* (Checklist #243)

Below:
*Daughters of Rebecca Club, from Isabella
Rosenbach Vacation School scrapbook*
(Checklist #244)

D.O.R. CLUB
DAUGHTERS OF REBECCA
NUMBER CHILDREN ON ROLL 37

What Our Name Means To Us

The name Rebecca brings to
our mind two great ladies in Jewish
history.
The first lady having been the wife
of Isaac who was kind and as our
BIBLE tells us, the Mother of
thousands and ten thousands.
Then Rebecca Gratz who founded
our fine Sunday School and who
worked long and hard to instill into Jewish children a desire to
learn more of our forefathers
and to make us better Jews.

249. **Third Annual Purim Ball,
West Philadelphia
Hebrew School,**
19 March, 1939
Broadside, 11 1/2″ x 14″
Philadelphia Jewish Archives
Center at the Balch
Institute. Gift of United
Hebrew Schools and
Yeshivas

250. **Annual Picnic of the Beth
Israel Religious School,**
c. 1940
Photograph by Jacob
Stelman, 10″ x 8″
Harriet Joyce Epstein

251. **Philadelphia School
District notice to
parents,** posted in high
schools in predominantly
Jewish neighborhoods,
March, 1940
Printed on paper in Yiddish,
11″ x 8 1/2″
Philadelphia Jewish Archives
Center at the Balch
Institute. Gift of Manfried
Mauskopf

111

Business and Commerce

252. **Levy's Dry Goods Store**,
    1857
    Lithograph, 19 3/4″ x 26 1/2″
    Historical Society of
    Pennsylvania

253. **S. Tobias Wines and
    Liquors**, 1846
    Lithograph, 12 1/2″ x 18 1/2″
    Library Company of
    Philadelphia

254. ***Baxter's Panoramic
    Business Directory,
    Third Street from Arch to
    Market,*** east side, 1860
    Lithograph, 20″ x 16″
    Library Company of
    Philadelphia

255. **Lit Brothers, Industrial
    Exposition,** Philadelphia,
    1908
    Photographic postcard,
    5 1/2″ x 3 1/2″
    Atwater Kent Museum

256. **Lit Brothers-sponsored
    picnic in the park,** early
    20th century
    Photograph, 9 1/4″ x 6″
    Philadelphia Jewish Archives
    Center at the Balch
    Institute. Steyer
    Family Collection. Gift of
    Mr. and Mrs. Harry Moss

257. **The Lit Brothers' Store,**
    Philadelphia
    Color postcard,
    5 1/4″ x 3 1/2″
    Atwater Kent Museum

Right:
Department store post cards (Checklist #266,
#257, and #255)

Snellenburg's Market, 11th to 12th Street,
Philadelphia, Pa.

The Lit Brother's Store, Philadelphia, Pa.

"HYDEGRADE" Booth Industrial Exposition 1908.
LIT BROTHERS.   Philadelphia, Pa.

258. **4 Women's hats from Millinery Salon, Lit Brothers,** c. 1940
a) Synthetic,
   9″ (diam.) x 2 1/2″
b) Synthetic,
   9 1/2″ x 8 1/2″ x 3″
c) Synthetic,
   7 1/2″ (diam.) x 4 1/2″
d) Linen and satin ribbon,
   9 1/2″ x 7 3/4″ x 3″
Atwater Kent Museum

259. **Lit Brothers hat box,** c. 1940
Cardboard, 17″ x 17″ x 6″
Atwater Kent Museum

260. **Toiletries owned by Rosa Lit**
Glass and plastic. Decals with initials "RLL"
Clock: 3″ x 3″ x 1/2″
2 Perfume bottles:
   2″ x 1″ x 3 1/4″
Hairbrush: 6″ x 1 1/4″ x 1 1/4″
2 Cosmetic jars:
   2 1/4″ (diam.) x 1 1/4″
Oval cosmetic jar:
   2 3/4″ x 2″ × 3 1/8″
Atwater Kent Museum

261. **Gimbel Brothers warehouse fire, 20th and Market Streets,** c. 1918
Photograph, 4 1/2″ x 6 1/2″
Atwater Kent Museum

Above:
Bronze Gimbel Brothers sign (Checklist #262)

Above:
Kosher food riots, 1917 (Checklist #269)

262. Gimbel Brothers Department Store sign
Bronze, 30″ x 20″ x 1 1/2″
Atwater Kent Museum

263. View of 4th Street on market day, early 20th century
Photograph, 6 1/2″ x 4 3/8″
Urban Archives Center, Temple University. Octavia Hill Association Collection

264. #304 South Street looking west, early 20th century
Photograph, 10″ x 8″
Philadelphia City Archives

265. N. Snellenburg and Co., 5th, South and Passyunk Aves., Philadelphia
Lithograph by Burk and McFetridge, 27 3/4″ x 21 3/4″
Balch Museum Collection. Museum Purchase

266. Snellenberg's Market, 11th to 12th Streets, 1912
Color postcard, 5 1/2″ x 3 1/2″
Atwater Kent Museum

267. "Printing Done at the Lowest Prices"
Advertising sign in English and Yiddish, 20″ x 13″
Philadelphia Jewish Archives Center at the Balch Institute. Gift of Jerome Keiser

268. Green Brothers Pure Food Market, Philadelphia
"Every Egg is Guaranteed 21 cents a Dozen"
Photographic postcard, 5 3/8″ x 3 3/8″
Philadelphia Jewish Archives Center at the Balch Institute. Theodore and Esther Green Collection. Gift of Mollie G. Fischer

269. **Kosher Food Riots, South Philadelphia,** 23 February, 1917
Photograph, 10″ x 8″
Philadelphia Evening Bulletin/Temple Urban Archives

270. **The United Push Carts Peddlers Association meeting at 329 Pine Street,** 4 June, 1922
Broadside, 8 3/8″ x 10 3/4″
Philadelphia Jewish Archives Center at the Balch Institute. Gift of Anne Green

271. **Marshall Street curb market north from 907 N. Marshall,** 7 September, 1925
Photograph, 10″ x 8″
Philadelphia City Archives

272. **Kosher Slaughterer's notice of price increase,** 1928
Printed on paper in English and Yiddish, 8 1/2″ x 10 7/8″
Philadelphia Jewish Archives Center at the Balch Institute. Abraham Hofferman Papers. Gift of Mrs. Abraham Hofferman

273. **"Stern the Caterer" truck,** 1934
Photograph by Simon A. Gilbert, 11 1/2″ x 8 1/4″
Philadelphia Jewish Archives Center at the Balch Institute

274. **View of 4th Street south of Monroe,** 1936
Photograph, 10″ x 8″
Philadelphia City Archives

275. **Famous 4th Street Delicatessen, 4th and Bainbridge Streets,** 1933
Photograph, 10″ x 8″
Auspitz Family

276. **"Old Original Bookbinder's Restaurant," 2nd and Chestnut Streets,** 1938
Photograph, 9 7/8″ x 8″
Taxin Family

277. **Apron salesman, 2nd and Fitzwater Streets,** 1938
Photograph, 10″ x 8″
Philadelphia Evening Bulletin/Temple Urban Archives

278. **Margulis storefront,** 1930s
Photograph, 7 1/2″ x 9 1/4″
National Museum of American Jewish History. Gift of Harriet Braunfeld

279. **Bayuk cigar box,** c. 1933-35
Tin, 7 1/4″ x 3″ x 5 1/4″
Balch Museum Collection. Museum Purchase

Below:
Famous 4th Street Delicatessen (Checklist #275)

Above:
Portrait of David Braginsky (Checklist #289)

Labor and Work Reform

280. Singer Sewing Machine,
c. 1910
Cast iron, 45″ x 14″ x 28″
Arch Sewing Machine
Company

**281. Buttonhole cutter for
men's suits and coats,**
early 20th century
Cast iron, 14″ x 16″ x 14″
Arch Sewing Machine
Company

**282. "Demand a Living Wage,"
Philadelphia,** c. 1915
Broadside by United Printing
Company in Yiddish,
9″ x 12″
Urban Archives Center,
Temple University

**283. "Shiplakoff, Socialist
Assemblyman in Phila."**
(General Organizer of the
Amalgamated Clothing
Workers of America),
Philadelphia, 14 August
1916
Broadside by United Printing
Company in English,
Italian and Yiddish,
12 1/4″ x 18 1/2″
Urban Archives Center,
Temple University

**284. Workmen's Circle, 575
Peretz Branch,
Philadelphia,** 1916
Photograph by the
Rembrandt Studio,
12″ x 9 1/4″
Philadelphia Jewish Archives
Center at the Balch
Institute. Gift of Mrs. Pearl
B. Olanoff

**285. "Cutting Our Wages Means
Nothing Less Than
Cutting Our Throats,"
International Ladies
Garment Workers Union,**
Waist and Dressmakers'
Union of Philadelphia,
Local No. 15
Broadside, 16″ x 19 7/8″
Philadelphia Jewish Archives
Center at the Balch
Institute. Gift of the
International Ladies
Garment Workers Union

**286. "Bessie's first job in
America at the paper box
factory"**
Photograph attributed to
Benjamin Mednick, 11″ x 8″
Clare Lewin and Seymour
Mednick

**287. Soup pot used by Isadore
(Itzak) Mayer to
transport cold soup to
work at Brown's Knitting
Mills,** c. 1920
Enamel, 6″ (diam.) x 6″
Balch Museum Collection.
Gift of Mrs. Philip Miller

**288. International Workers
Order, BR #30, Jewish
Section, Philadelphia**
Photograph, 9 7/8″ x 18″
Philadelphia Jewish Archives
Center at the Balch
Institute. Gift of William
Uris

289. David Braginsky, 1932
Photograph, 11″ x 14″
Terry Horowitz

**290. Pen inscribed "Presented
by W.[est] P.[hiladelphia]
Jewish Branch
S.[ocialist] P.[arty] to
Mrs. D. Braginsky,"**
5″ x 1/2″ (diam.)
Balch Museum Collection.
Workmen's Circle
(Philadelphia District)
Collection

291. **Immigrant garment workers,** 1930's
Photograph, 10 1/8″ x 8″
Urban Archives Center,
Temple University

292. **Ball Committee, Amalgamated Clothing Workers of America,**
Finishers and Buttonhole Makers Local 156, 1st Annual Dance, Broadwood Hotel, 28 February 1936
Photograph by Roma Studio, 19 7/8″ x 10″
Urban Archives Center,
Temple University

293. **Amalgamated Clothing Workers charter,**
Wholesale Clothing Clerks Union, Local 375, Philadelphia, 1940
Printed on paper, 19″ x 24″
Urban Archives Center,
Temple University

In Search of a Haven

294. **Minute book, Alliance Israelite Universelle,**
1868-1934
Bound notebook, 15 3/4″ x 13″
Philadelphia Jewish Archives Center at the Balch Institute. Gift of Federation of Jewish Agencies

295. **Stock certificate, The Jewish Colonial Trust,**
8 July, 1901
Printed on paper, 14 3/8″ x 9 1/8″
Philadelphia Jewish Archives Center at the Balch Institute. Gift of William B. Soble

296. **Manuel F. Lisan's Delegate's Credential to the Eighth Annual Convention of the Federation of American Zionists,** at Touro Hall, Philadelphia, 16-20 June, 1905
Printed card, 6 1/2″ x 4 3/4″
Philadelphia Jewish Archives Center at the Balch Institute. Gift of Manuel F. Lisan

297. **"Remember the National Fund," commemorating the 10th Annual Convention of the Federation of American Zionists,**
1 July, 1907
Postcard, 5 1/2″ x 3″
Philadelphia Jewish Archives Center at the Balch Institute. Gift of Manuel F. Lisan

298. **Notice of a Mass Meeting sponsored by the Maccabeans at Poale Tzedek Synagogue,**
1011-19 South 5th Street, Philadelphia, 27 March 1910
Printed on paper in Yiddish, 6″ x 9″
Philadelphia Jewish Archives Center at the Balch Institute. Gift of Manuel F. Lisan

Left:
Immigrant garment workers (Checklist #291)

299. **Jewish National Fund Land Donation Certificate presented to Emanuel (sic) F. Lisan by the Maccabean Zion Society of Philadelphia,** 25 December 1912
Printed on paper, 16" x 12"
Philadelphia Jewish Archives Center at the Balch Institute. Gift of Manuel F. Lisan

300. *The Young Judean*, **"A Magazine for the Zionist Youth,"** New York, July, 1919
Journal, 6 1/8" x 9 1/16"
Philadelphia Jewish Archives Center at the Balch Institute. Isaac E. Feinstein Papers. Gift of Harriet Baskin

301. **Philadelphia Young Judea Leaders with organization president Isaac E. Feinstein,** c. 1920-21
Photograph, 10" x 8"
Philadelphia Jewish Archives Center at the Balch Institute. Isaac E. Feinstein Papers. Gift of Harriet Baskin

302. **American Jewish Relief Appeal,** 29 January - 6 February, 1922
Poster, 22" x 32"
National Museum of American Jewish History. Gift of Edwin Wolf 2nd

303. *The Romance of a People*, **supplement to** *The Evening Ledger*, **Philadelphia,** February, 1934
Printed on paper, 11 3/16" x 16 1/8"
Philadelphia Jewish Archives Center at the Balch Institute. Gift of Anne Smilowitz

304. *The Romance of a People*, **a musical and dramatic benefit for the settlement of German-Jewish Refugees in Palestine,** at Convention Hall, 19 February - 3 March, 1938
Printed program, 9" x 12"
Maxwell Whiteman Collection

305. **Certificate of commendation for Harry Berger, Allied Jewish Appeal of Philadelphia,** 1938
Printed on paper, 12" x 9"
Balch Museum Collection

Below:
Jewish National Fund Land Donation Certificate (Checklist #299)

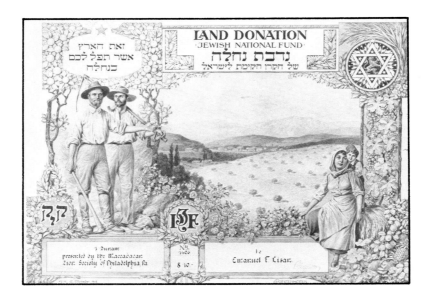

Above (Color Plate #1):
Parokhet *(ark cover) from Hevra Tehillim-B'nai Israel* (Checklist #51)

Above (Color Plate #2):
Window from Keneseth Israel Synagogue (Checklist #49)

Above (Color Plate #3):
Polish menorah (Checklist #130)

Left (Color Plate #4):
Leaded glass door from the Great Romanian Synagogue
(Checklist #55)

Above (Color Plate #5):
Wimple from Germany (Checklist #38)

Right (Color Plate #6):
Tallit *bag, c. 1890* (Checklist #58)

Below (Color Plate #7):
Shofar *and bag from the Great Romanian Synagogue*
(Checklist #52)

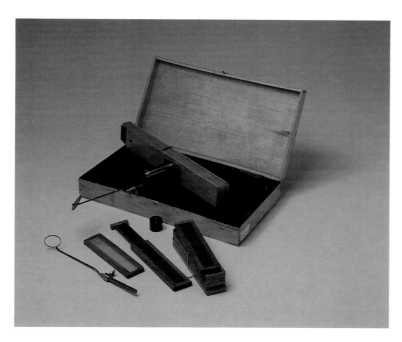

Above (Color Plate #8):
Laryngeal camera invented by Dr. Jacob da Silva Solis-Cohen (Checklist #127)

Below (Color Plate #9):
Tallit *and* tefillin *with bags* (Checklist #64 and #57)

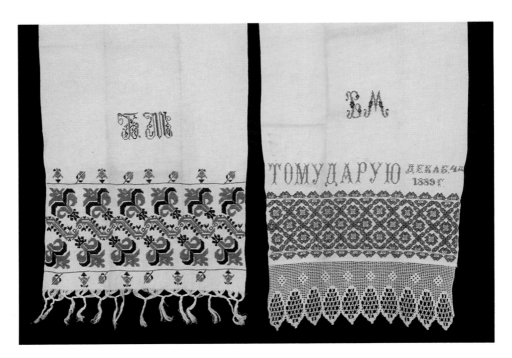

Above (Color Plate #10):
Russian embroidered cloths (Checklist #137 and #136)

Right (Color Plate #11):
Doily made in Young Women's Union sewing class (Checklist #94)

Left (Color Plate #12):
Beltz-Bessarabia commemorative anniversary plate
(Checklist #75)

Below (Color Plate #13):
Russian bowl and pot (Checklist #140 and #139)

Above (Color Plate #14):
Ukrainian miniature samovar set (Checklist #17)

Right (Color Plate #15):
Russian samovar (Checklist #13)

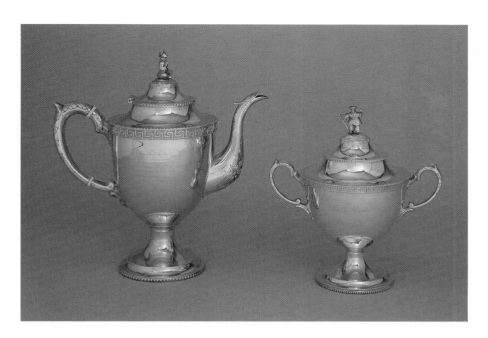

Above (Color Plate #16):
Coffee pot and sugar bowl presented to Rev. Jacob Frankel (Checklist #112)

Below (Color Plate #17):
Silver spice tower (Checklist #42), kiddush *cup* (Checklist #63), *ewer*
(Checklist #132) *and* omer *calendar* (Checklist #46)

Above (Color Plate #18):
A South Philadelphia Jew *by Joseph Sacks* (Checklist #20)

Above (Color Plate #19):
N. Snellenburg and Co. lithograph (Checklist #265)

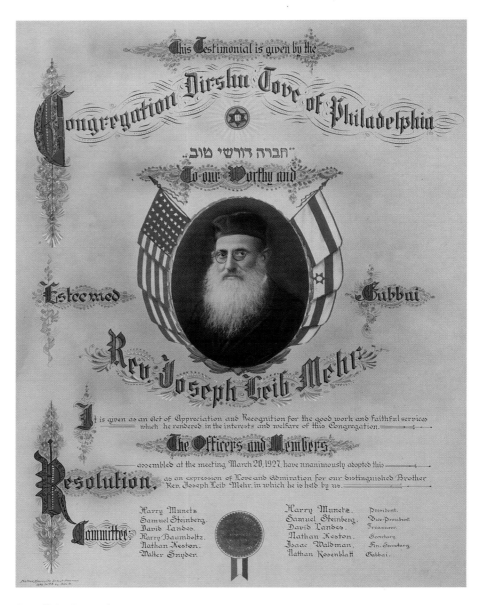

Above (Color Plate #20):
Testimonial to Rev. Joseph Leib Mehr (Checklist #60)

Above (Color Plate #21):
Memorial plaque for Sarah Rosner (Checklist #53)

Right (Color Plate #22):
Testimonial to Mr. and Mrs. Charles Cylinder (Checklist #80)

Above (Color Plate #23):
Labor strike poster (Checklist #282)

דיא גרינדער פון חברה תהלים :

מרדכי זאב בר צבי דוב שווארץ

יוסף בר ישראל וועקסלער

ברוך בן ציון בר אליעזר מגיד

מרדכי בר משה שיינקמאן

שאול בר מנשה דיכטער

נפתלי צבי בר יעקב יהודה ווייס

גרשון בר אליהו קרובץ

אהרן בר זאב סאסנאווסקי

יעקב זעליג בר משה פעסין

ניסן בר תנחום וויען

מרדכי ליב בר שלום פארכמאן

מרדכי בר ליב הלוי לעוויצקי

אברהם יעקב בר שמואל ניגאף

דוד בר ישראל צבי הלוי פארטער

שבתי בר משה ראוונער

Above (Color Plate #24):
Record book, Chevra Ateres Israel Anshe Brahin V'Choimetsch (Checklist #62)

133

Left (Color Plate #25):
Arch Street Theatre poster (Checklist #210)

Below (Color Plate #26):
Program for Romance of a People (Checklist #304)

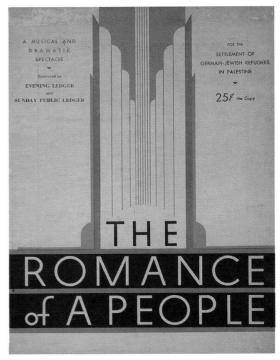

134